JN034209

Figures for Part 2

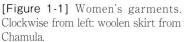

[Figure 1-1] Women's garments.
Clockwise from left: woolen skirt from
Chamula.
[Figure 1-2] huipil from San Andrés
Larráinzar.
[Figure 1-3] woolen shirt from
Chamula.
[Figure 1-4] huipil from Magdalenas.
Photo by Gracia Imberton Deneke

[Figure 2]
Men's garments. Gray woolen vest from Chamula, colorful woolen vest from Zinacantán, cotton shirt from Huixtán. Photo by Gracia Imberton Deneke

[Figure 3]
Indigenous market in the exconvent of Santo Domingo, San Cristóbal de Las Casas. Photo by Gracia Imberton Deneke

[Figure 4]
Textil Center of the Mayan World in the exconvent of Santo Domingo. Photo courtesy by José Luis Escalona

[Figure 5]
Fashion design store in a shopping center.
Photo by Gracia Imberton Deneke

[Figure 6]
Traditional hand-made clothing in Wenshan, China.
Photo courtesy by Chie Miyawaki

[Figure 7]
New Styles of Hmong Outfit in Wenshan, China.
Photo courtesy by Chie Miyawaki

Figures for Part 3

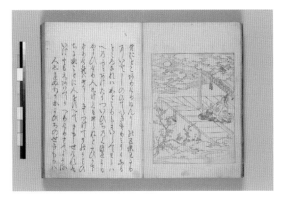

[Figure 1]
Isemonogatari, Dataset of Pre-Modern Japanese Text, owned by National Institute of Japanese Literature.
BIBLIO ID:200023067,DOI:10.20730/200023067

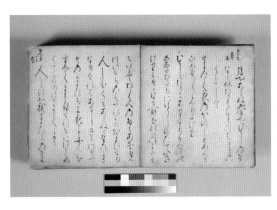

[Figure 2]
Isemonogatari, Dataset of Pre-Modern Japanese Text, owned by National Institute of Japanese Literature.
BIBLIO ID:200024135, DOI:10.20730/200024135

[Figure 3]
Board for printing, *Kagami-Jinja Yuraiki* , owned by Kagami-Jinja.
Photo by Koko Nango

[Figure 4-1]
Clelia Marchi holding her bed sheet.
Photo courtesy by Clelia Marchi's heirs Livi

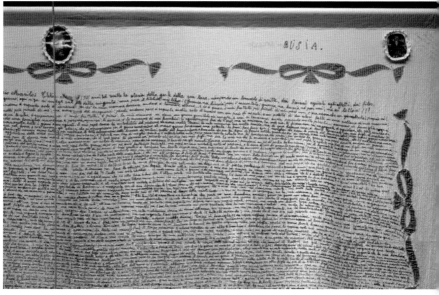

[Figure 4-2]
Marchi's sheet. Creative Commons.(CC BY 3.0)

Materialism of Archive
記録のマテリアリズム

A Dialogue on Movement / Migration and Things
Between Japanese and Mexican Researchers

ー移動／移民とモノをめぐる日墨研究者による対話ー

Edited by Hiroki Ogasawara and Fumiko Sukikara

Table of Contents

記録のマテリアリズム―本書について

　本書は「記録のマテリアリズム」をテーマに 2019 年 11 月 10 日に開催され
た国際合同シンポジウムの記録である。このシンポジウムは、神戸大学国際文
化学研究推進センター（PROMIS）と、メキシコ・チアパス自治大学先住民研
究所との学術交流協定締結を契機に、今後の共同研究の出発点として開催され
た。グラシア・インベルトン・デネケ教授（マヤ系先住民の生活誌、チアパス
自治大学）、ホセ・ルイス・エスカロナ・ヴィクトリア教授（先住民村落の社
会・政治研究、メキシコ社会人類学高等研究院）、鋤柄史子氏（マヤの文化翻
訳、バルセロナ大学社会人類学専攻博士課程）をメキシコから招聘し、アジア
各地の伝統染織の生産地で調査をしてきた中谷文美教授（岡山大学）、移民研
究者のジャンルカ・ガッタ准教授（神戸大学国際連携推進機構国際教育総合セ
ンターおよび国際文化学研究科）を討論者に迎えた当シンポジウムには、研究
者、学生、一般含めのべ 50 人以上が参加した。まず参加者の皆さんに深く感
謝を申し上げることから始めたい。

　シンポジウムのテーマである「記録のマテリアリズム」と、会場となった神
戸海外移住と文化の交流センターとの関係について述べておきたい。ブラジル
をはじめとするラテンアメリカ諸国に移住する人々を健康診断、ポルトガル語
の基礎知識習得、ごく基礎的な農業知識の習得などを目的として収容する施設
として、この建造物は 1928 年に建てられた。現在は神戸市の指定管理施設と
して日伯協会、C.A.P 芸術と計画会議、そして CBK 関西ブラジル人コミュニ
ティの 3 団体が使用している。

　特に CBK は、日系ブラジル人の言葉や生活面での支援をしている NPO で、
その活動の中でも移住してから 3 世代、4 世代目の子どもや若者を対象とした
日本語とポルトガル語の教室を開いている点が重要だ。家庭ではポルトガル語
で、学校では日本語で、言語アイデンティティのゆらぎをダイレクトに経験す
る子どもたちに学びの場を提供しているからだ。そのような活動を行っている
団体が集うこの建物でシンポジウムを開くことが、主催者である私たちにとっ
てはとても意味のあることだった。それはこの場所に、文化が交差し混交しあ

う風景が描写されるからであり、その風景は、かつても、そして今も移民する人々によって作られているからだ。

　私たちは、一つの関心を共有している。それは移動である。移民として語られる人間のみならず、モノの移動も重要な関心事なのだ。モノという日本語は、英語にすると複数の言葉に変化する。オブジェクト（対象）、マテリアル（材質／物質）、者、物。こうした多様で多方向なモノの性質を、このメンバーで多角的に議論しあいたい。

　このアイデアは、私たち神戸大学 PROMIS の研究メンバーと、チアパス自治大学の知的交流から芽生えたものである。より具体的には、神戸大学国際文化学部を卒業後、同大学院人間発達学研究科で修士号を獲得した鋤柄史子さんが、その後チアパス自治大学の先住民研究所修士課程に入学したことから全てが始まった。2017 年秋のことだ。彼女のチアパスでの指導教員が、インベルトン・デネケ教授とエスカロナ・ヴィクトリア教授 だった。2017 年の秋、鋤柄さんの尽力によって小笠原が三人の住むサン・クリストバル・デ・ラスカサス市を訪れ、ワークショップを開催させてもらった。その際に、インベルトン・デネケ教授との懇談の席で、学術交流をさらに拡大したいということで話がまとまり、1 年後の 2018 年 12 月、PROMIS の研究チームがサン・クリストバルを訪れ、国際ワークショップを共同開催した。そのメンバーの一人だった南郷晃子さんは、2019 年 2 月 3 月に若手女性研究者支援の助成金により、チアパス自治大学での研究に従事することができた。このように、私たちの知的学術的交流はすでに実質的に始まっており、本シンポジウムは船出であると同時に、それぞれの研究の現在形を確認し、次世代の研究者を巻き込みながら今後の展開へと道筋をつけることを目的としたものでもあった。

　私たちに共通のテーマは、モノである。モノ。モノについては、2，3 の一般的なアプローチの仕方があるだろう。第 1 に、フェティシズムである。モノはすぐに私たちの手を離れ、願望や欲望の代補として機能する。第 2 に、アニミズム的と言ってもよいであろうモノへの視座がある。モノは人間からだけではなく、モノ同士でそれぞれ意味を担い、独立した意味世界を形成するようになる。第 3 に、単純に唯物論的な考え方だ。人間の意図や関心とは一切関係なく、モノはすでにそこにある。客観的な実在として、ある。私たちの意図以前

に存在するのがモノであり、私たちはそのモノを意図通りに操ることなどできないという考え方だ。

　どれか一つが真理であり正しいということなどできず、どれか一つが他よりも優れた視点であるということもできない。多様なモノへの視座を交差させ、織り交ぜ、区別したり混同したりしながら私たちは世界との関係を取り結んでいる。しかしながら、モノは近年ますます雄弁に私たちに何かを訴えるようになってきた。自然、環境、他者の持ち物、他者の身体、他性の具現化、近代性、交通、移民、これらは全て、モノを伴うグローバル・スケールの移動の問題として考えられるだろう。だから、モノも動くという視点を持たなければならない。モノは人間とともに、また同時に人間の動きとは関係ない方向に動き、人間の意思や意図に沿わないどころか、それらに抗い、逆撫で、無視するのである。

　なぜモノが重要なのか。なぜモノについて真摯に考えなければならないのか。例えば、モノはときに舌よりも雄弁に語る。沈黙という雄弁さも含めて、語る。この雄弁さは、人間の口から発せられる言葉を通じた雄弁さとは似ても似つかない。モノは何も喋らず、ただそこにあるだけなのに、何かを強烈に語りかけてくることがあるのもまた、事実なのだ。三部構成となる本書には、このようなモノへの基本的な認識を共有した人類学者、社会学者、説話文学研究者、そしてカルチュラル・スタディーズの研究者が、それぞれの視点から展開した研究発表や応答に対し、多くの参加者を巻き込んだ実に闊達な、長い一日の議論が収められている。

　パート1「記録（archive）のメディア性」は、ホセ・ルイス・エスカロナ・ヴィクトリアによる「政治的認識論と現代世界の形成（Political Epistemology and the Making of the Contemporary World）」と題する報告から始まる。エスカロナ・ヴィクトリアは、「モノ」が「記録」となる特定の過程で帯びる価値と意味を決定する物質性の枠組み（frame）が存在することを検証する。この枠組みが現代世界の認識のあり方をどのように形成してきたのか、博物館などの事例を引きながら理論的考察を進めている。それに対しコメンテーターのジャンルカ・ガッタは、その枠組の権力から離れるためにカオスへと戻ることを提唱し、フロアとの熱気ある意見交換や議論も含めて実に論争的で刺激的な場面が作り出された。

5

パート2「移動する / 交差文化的な記憶のマテリアリズム」は、インベル
トン・デネケの報告「織布、記憶、文化の商品化（Textiles, Memory and
Commodification of Culture）」から始まる。インベルトン・デネケは、商品（モ
ノ）として流通し消費されるために生産される先住民のテキスタイルが、同時
に民族アイデンティティを表象するシンボルとしても機能している現状を踏ま
えたうえで、はたして商品化されたモノは記憶を内在しうるのだろうかと問う。
この問いかけに応答するのはコメンテーターの中谷文美である。参加者との議
論では、先住民の位置づけをめぐって積極的な意見交換が行われた。
　シンポジウムの最後のセッションの記録がパート3である。これまでに登壇
した四名によって行われた議論について、若手研究者二名（鋤柄史子と南郷晃
子）が各々の興味関心に近づけながらコメントする、ラウンド・ディスカッシ
ョンである。議論の内容の豊かさに加えて、ヴェテラン研究者たちの場慣れた
プレゼンテーションに対して、若手の研究者が自分たちの研究テーマを積極的
にぶつけ、次世代へとたすきを繋げる対話を生み出すことで、本シンポジウム
本来の目的に沿う議論の場となった。
　本書の主たる言語は英語である。それは、シンポジウム自体が全て英語で行
われたからという実際的な理由もあるが、メキシコからの参加者が読むことが
でき、できるだけ多くの読者に目を通してもらうためには英語に頼らざるをえ
ないという事情もある。実際の議論の現場では英語に加え日本語、スペイン語、
イタリア語が飛び交うというバベル的なカオスを経験することもできたが、そ
の場合はそのままの言語で記述してある箇所もある。しかし、記録するという
主旨のもとでは、できるだけ英語に統一し、補助的な意味で各部に日本語での
概要を付した。
　しかし、これは参加者の間でも議論になったことだが、英語をそのままグロ
ーバル言語として受け入れ、そのヘゲモニーを無条件に認めたというわけでは
ない。主催者としては、スペイン語と日本語話者にイタリア語話者が加わると
いう構成で、誰の母語でもない第3言語である英語が、誰からも等距離にあっ
て遠い言語だという判断があったということである。先住民の布や文物がテー
マとなった場面があるのに、先住民の言語ではないどころか、先住民の参加者
が一人もいないという大きな問題も抱えたままである。それはメキシコ先住民

に限った話ではなく、ところどころで話題になったアイヌに関する論点も同じことだ。

　だれのモノを、だれの言葉で語るのか。単一の正解を求めることは不可能だ。すでに所有格で固定できるほど、領有の確定された話ではないからである。しかし、領有の融解や重複だけではなく、再領有化をも視野に入れた人類学や社会調査を考える時、このモノと言語との関係性は避けて通ってはいけない問題である。モノは簡単に再領有される。そしてまた同じくらい簡単に所有の手をすり抜ける。移動とは線条的な差異の痕跡をたどることではなく、領有と再領有の反復のさらなる繰り返しであり、そこで生じる折衝のあり方なのだ。

　解決よりも課題を、オチを付けることよりも今後につながる問題を残すことを。こうした観点からすれば、シンポジウムは大成功であったと言ってよい。新型コロナ・ウィルスによるパンデミックは、本シンポジウムの主要テーマであった移動の様相、意味、あり方、認識の仕方をそれぞれ大きく変容させようとしている。これまでの移動の理解が無意味化するということではないだろう。それはそれで残るとしても、私たちが今後どのような対象をどのように追うことができるのか。そして、私たちはまたこのテーマのもとで、どのように出会うことができるのか。オンラインで、と手続き的に済ませるわけにはいかないだろう。それでは、同じモノをともに手に取ることができないからだ。少なくとも現状の技術によってそれはまだ、不可能である。新たな出会いのあり方を模索する時間はまだまだ続くだろう。期せずして、モノは新たなチャレンジを課してきている。

　本書のもとになったシンポジウムは、PROMIS2019 年度研究プロジェクト「記録のマテリアリズム：『モノ』、移動／移民、ナラティヴの領域横断的研究」（研究代表者：小笠原博毅）の一環として開催された。PROMIS、ならびにシンポジウムに参加していただいた栢木清吾 PROMIS 研究員、神戸大学国際文化学研究科の辛島理人、井上弘貴両准教授のおかげで開催が実現した。また 2019年度神戸大学先端融合研究環人文・社会科学系融合研究領域ワークショップ経費助成金を開催経費の一部とするために、同研究環および坂井一成教授にご助力いただいた。そして本書の出版は、岡田浩樹 PROMIS センター長のご助言によって獲得できた PROMIS 出版補助費のおかげで可能となった。皆様に記

して深く感謝申し上げます。（小笠原博毅）

シンポジウムの記録

Introduction

Seigo Kayanoki: Thank you very much for coming today to our international symposium. I'm Seigo Kayanoki, research fellow of Research Center for Promoting Intercultural Studies, PROMIS, which is of Kobe University. I'm the moderator here. First of all, I have some announcements. If you haven't yet enrolled at that reception, please write your name and email address, or something like that, in break time. And the second announcement is about language. I think you already understand today's symposium will be held in English.

So this symposium, this international symposium entitled Materialism of Archive, is held collaboratively by Institute of Indigenous Studies of Autonomous University of Chiapas, Mexico and PROMIS of Kobe University. I would like to thank especially Professor Gracia Imberton Deneke from Autonomous University of Chiapas and José Luis Escalona Victoria from Center for Research and Postgraduate Studies in Social Anthropology, who kindly accepted our invitation, to come to Japan and present their research projects to us. And also I would like to thank Professor Ayami Nakatani and Professor Gianluca Gatta to serve as a commentator to our symposium.

So, before starting the symposium, Professor Hirotaka Inoue, who is vice-director of PROMIS, will give the welcome speech on behalf of organisers of this event, so please.

Hirotaka Inoue: Good morning guys. Buenos días. おはようございます。 Zǎoshang hǎo. On behalf of the Research Centre for Promoting Intercultural Studies, I would like to thank Professor Ogasawara for organizing a beautiful and wonderful joint international symposium collaborated by IEI and Kobe University. And I also want to thank Professor Gracia Imberton Deneke and Professor José Luis Escalona Victoria, for coming to Japan, coming to Kobe to join their symposium and programs. We, the Center for Promoting Intercultural Studies, have four divisions and support research programs and symposium every year, and we also support young researchers for promoting intercultural studies and other research fields. So, I hope you all enjoy the joint symposium today. Thank you so much.

Kayanoki: So next, Professor Hiroki Ogasawara of Kobe University will talk about the subject and agenda of this symposium. So Please.

Hiroki Ogasawara: Good morning everyone. Buenos días. Well, Seigo and Hirotaka expressed our sincere thanks to those guest speakers, commentators and all of you who take part in this event. Thank you very much. I'm also really grateful to you all for coming here, because this is a place where this kind of event has to be conceived. I already explained to you this morning in our briefing meeting. It's about a historical place, not only for those who used this building as a crossing point to emigrate to Brazil as well as Latin-American countries, but that was actually long time ago, nowadays this is more kind of contemporary use for Japanese-Brazilians who have some difficulties living in this country, particularly for the kids, you know, second and third generation's Japanese-Brazilian kids who immigrated to this country, but they have some difficulties in classrooms, schools, including family houses, because you know, language is slightly kind of obstacle for them to live, in other words, to be "assimilated" to the culture, in Japan. So some kids are learning Portuguese here, their parents are learning Japanese here. I deliberately take in only one function of this building, but other things are going on, but it's really important for us to think about this kind of cultural mixing, cultural crossings, scenes, you know, atmosphere. The air of this building produces ever since, let's say 1928 when this building was built.

I'm saying this because we share common interest in something that relates to migration. Not only the migration of human beings, but migration of things as well. Things, the thing and " モノ " in Japanese, but if you turned your head to English, " モノ " can be translatable to any ideas like objects, it's translated into

Japanese as " モ ノ ". Material also can be " モ ノ ". Only one Japanese word " モ ノ " means at least three or four different English ideas. So I think we can, you know, be able to hold on together this diverse aspects of " モ ノ " in one place here. Then we have ideal guests from Mexico, Gracia, José Luis and, Fumiko actually. This event today, the seed of this event, actually, was sown when she joined the Autonomous University of Chiapas, when?

Fumiko Sukikara: 20…17? I don't know.

Ogasawara: 2016? 17?

Gracia Imberton Deneke: 2017 to 2018.

Ogasawara: Actually Fumiko studied for master's degree with the guidance of Gracia and José Luis in Chiapas. Since she joined them, things were happening in a way. First, she kindly invited me to come to San Cristóbal, Chiapas, to give a talk the same year she joined the Autonomous University of Chiapas, in 2017. A year later our delegation from Kobe went to Chiapas and Mexico City as well. It was last December, almost one year ago. Then we successfully invited both of you, and you, come to Kobe. And another thing, Nango-san, is she arriving? Ah yes. Koko spent a couple of months in Chiapas last February and March to conduct a research. So we have intellectual exchanges, have been really active since two or three years ago. So this opportunity is a kind of pinnacle, a combination of intellectual exchanges.

And then we have found common interests in things " モ ノ ". Thinking about things, I think, as far as I'm concerned, we have two or three different perspectives regarding how to think about things. The first perspective will be a kind of feticism. Things can be active without our hands. Things can have, you know, their own meanings. It's a kind of substitution for our desire or wish. The second perspective could be animistic, more animistic way of thinking. Things have their own ways. Things have their own meanings, independent meaning, independent from human beings. Third perspective would be really really simply a materialistic idea. Things are out there, without any concern from ours. Things out there, objectively. We can't touch things because things exist prior to our intension. It's very very materialistic.

I don't think, you know, we can choose one of them. I don't think one of those is more superior to others. You know, I don't think so. But, we have to be open to these variable aspects when it comes to think about things. But today particularly things are concerned with modernization, movements, transfers, migrations. Movement. Things move. And things remain there to say something to us. Also things move to the other side, somewhere, then leave something for us to think about. You know, I'm not getting into more complicated kind of narratives because we will have excellent talks today. But I want you to be aware of this idea, things: why things are important. Why things can be, sometimes, far more eloquent than human voices: far more eloquent than our tongue. Including being silent. That is important, too. Eloquence doesn't come out of its eloquent sense. Sometimes things say nothing, just remain there, but really appealing to us. So it's going to be a really long day. From now to 5 o'clock in the evening. So yes, please be free to go to the bathroom, coffee is available just around there. And a convenience store is close in two or three minutes walk. So you know, this is a symposium but I don't want it to be very fixed, one way street lecture. I want it to be really kind, you know, I want it to be more open, flexible, gradual discussion. So any moment, if you have some questions, please raise your hand. Your intervention is always welcome. Ok, thank you.

Kayanoki: Thank you very much. From now we are moving to the first session and the title is "mediality of archive". So I want to pass my microphone to the chairperson of the first session. So please.

Part 1

—

Mediality of Archive

Part 1

Mediality of Archive

Hirotaka Inoue: Ok. Hello again. I'm Hirotaka Inoue, moderator of this first session. And I'm glad to be in charge of moderating. First I would like to introduce Professor José Luis Escalona Victoria. He owns the PhD in social anthropology from the University of Manchester, UK. And he is now professor at the Center of the Research And Advanced Study in Social Anthropology in Mexico (CIESAS). He published many articles; also he published a book titled Política en el Chiapas rural contemporáneo. Una aproximación etnográfica al poder (*Politics in Contemporary Rural Chiapas. An Ethnographical Approach for Power*). So it had been paying attention to the concept of power, I think. He published that book in 2009, and that was awarded the national Arturo Warman Prize. Arturo Warman is a legendary Mexican anthropologist to past away in to some degree. So, He first makes the presentation titled 'Political Epistemology and the Making of the Contemporary World'.

And after that, after he make that presentation, the Professor Gianluca Gatta will give us comment about the presentation, and almost everybody knows about him, but I would like to also introduce Professor Gatta. He is a project-associated professor at the Graduate School of Intercultural Studies and the Faculty of Global Human Sciences. And he specializes in anthropology and sociology on human mobility with an emphasis on the Euro-Mediterranean region. And also he is a founder and secretary of the Archive of Migrant Memories Association based in Rome. So we will start the session. I'm very honoured to begin with you, José. So let's get started.

José Luis Escalona Victoria
Political Epistemology and the Making of the Contemporary World
José Luis Escalona Victoria: Thank you. I want to thank the Research Center for Promoting Intercultural Studies (Promis) and its project representative: Dr. Hiroki Ogasawara, Ogasawara-san, as well as the Co-sponsor: Organization for Advanced and Integrated Research of Kobe University. Thank you very much. Thanks to all of you for being here. I'm glad to be here too. Let's start with objects. I'm going to read my presentation, but if you have questions, just raise your hand.

The world stands before our senses as a kind of a massive bunch of things, paraphrasing Marx's first words in *Das Capital*, in which the capitalist way of wealth appears as a collection of commodities[1]. I want to start by using the same image; however, instead of addressing the mode of production, I want to explore the mode of framing[2].

Things around us appear as a mass of different and irregularly delineated things, with a wide range of forms, colors, lights and intensities; noisily or silently, animated or unanimated, moving themselves following different rhythms and directions, endowed with the most diverse qualities, uses, impacts and meanings; and even, most of the time, unnoticed. This gathering of things also encompasses luminous and colorful images and signs, as well as sounds and lights, and we have even learned how to take them with us in screens of portable devices. They can change from being commodities to gifts, and then back again; from exchangeable values to unalienable items, from waste to treasure, and from irrelevant materials to highly priced pieces, charged with emotions; parts of ourselves.

Sometimes the things themselves seem to be disorganized, or at least to lack a clear organizing logic; they may even have chaotic discontinuities, without any anticipated purposes. In contrast, it is not uncommon for displays of things to follow combinations of directions and arrays. Thus, combinations of things vary as we move among them in real life or virtually, in in the company of other people or just on our lonely journey. Our daily experience of things depends on our routes among them, and on the types of items by themselves; however, that experience is strongly influenced by frames according to which they are arranged, ruled, allocated and exposed. In these cases, we can take them clearly as meaningful, useful or rightly allocated things. It is because of their allocation among other things than we can even take those things as if they were invisible, since we are used to their repeated and quiet presence in particular places. We also have special buildings that strongly suggest specific displays of things, like museums, archaeological parks and living historical towns, where different valuable dead and living things have either been stored and displayed, or else move themselves around. These architectures, like effect-making artefacts/architectures, are designed to produce multiple experiences[3] and eventually sensations[4].

The whole experience, which includes contact with things and animated corpses, is thus regulated in particular ways and situations. The spaces that are designed in such a way include scenarios for contemplation, education or pleasure, for tourists willing to learn about other people's lives around the world, in the present or in other times. There are, for instance, natural-history museums, where we can contemplate the natural world of stones, meteorites, minerals, sands and soils, or dissected plants and animals as whole units or in fragments, like skins, bones, and other body parts. There are also sculptures, drawings, paints or photos, or images in screens, holograms and avatars. All these things are exhibited in hierarchical schemes and timetables, as well as in linear or multilinear narratives, all of which order for us that which otherwise would be a bunch of multiple, contradictory and complex things. That order serves teachers, students or cultural tourists who are looking for explanations; or even visitors who might then finish the journey in a nearby garden or a restaurant, with an experience of having been learning something, and having seen some order brought out of chaos. Natural-history museums also offer another very interesting experience, as time-space travel machines. Some museums offer the experience of going far back in time, through different techniques of evocation—for example, even back to the moment of the very origin of the whole universe and time, the Big Bang—or to view the whole trajectory of life's evolution[5].

Expected and elicited effects of the ordering of chaos and of travel-like experiences are offered also by historical, archaeological and ethnological museums, as it has been pointed in different studies[6]. There are several mechanisms strategically employed to produce an effect of traveling through time and space; for example, through the display of objects in chronological order, through the exhibit of collections by epochal gatherings, and through the selection of the objects' qualities—no matter if pieces are spearheads, textiles or ceramics. That happens also with things displayed in clusters by world areas or places, so that the act of walking through them could be a simulacrum of travels through wider spaces and longer periods of time. Technologies for virtual trips are increasingly available, like the one that we can find in the Digital Museum in Copan Ruinas, Honduras. The town, founded in the 19th century in the *Departamento* (state) of Copan, received its name shortly after the first modern archaeological explorations of the ruined buildings of a nearby ancient city. Today, Copan Ruinas is a town with hotels, restaurants, shops and museums for visitors, because it is possible to visit the ruins of that ancient Central American city (which is now well known) via a short walking trip. But today visitors can just visit the place virtually, by using a computer and a screen at the Digital museum located right at the town's main square. This museum was built with the financial support of the Japanese Government and the scientific assistance of Tokyo's Kanazawa and Waseda Universities. Some images also show the architectures in their supposed original splendor. Another team from Harvard University has applied the same new digital techniques to recover the lost images of the famous hieroglyphic stairway built in the site of Copan. These technologies can then print the images to scale, to make it possible to read the text. It was a nice text written more than a thousand years ago, in a stairway in one of the main buildings; however, the blocks of the building collapsed, and some of them deteriorated to some point where it was impossible to recognize the scriptures written upon them. Thus, current new technologies allow people to reconstruct the building and make the text readable again[7]. In this way the past is molded in the present, and the exhibit gives the contemporary people an experience of the past (probably by working, also, as an artifice for producing the time-travel effect).

Archaeological sites and contemporary historical towns, even if they are not always clusters of things enclosed or separated from everyday life, are also embedded in such attempts to produce order and time-space travel effects. Visitors can move for a moment among walls, sculptures, gardens, bridges, houses and other architectures, and occasionally they can meet people wearing special clothes or garments to represent other places or times, to the point of producing the experience of otherness or alterity[8]. To me, these effects resemble those we experienced during our visit to Nishinomiya-Jinja Shrine, at the Hyogo prefecture, just before this conference. It was interesting in the same sense I am referring to here; yes, as tourists and worshipers are walking around, taking pictures and wearing costumes from different fashions and times[9]. In some cases, we cannot tell whether some parts of the spectacle are really designed as part of it, or for some locals; there is no division to be found between the quotidian life and the staging of things for visitors. This often happens, too, when touring indigenous villages in the Highland Chiapas, where I live. In a town called Zinacantan, for example, tourists visit homes to experience everyday life, sharing with local families their spaces, their patios and kitchens, where locals display the handmade craftwork (*artesanias*) and offer meals made of corn and beans. However, even if the experience appears to be a realistic deep contact with locals, part of the scenario is staged for tourists[10]. Seasonal fairs, where things are placed in public places during special days, to be exhibited, exchanged and sold, also produce a similar effect, by letting visitors enjoy the character of an epoch or a place.

We all know these things, so I will not go through more examples to make the point. What I want to stress now is that we in fact seem to enjoy these staged experiences of time-space oscillation; actually, we use them to get out of everyday life and chores (which are themselves embraced by certain rhythms and arrangements of things). In some way, these "cultural spaces" have techniques in common with theme parks, like Disneyland[11]. People are involved in a joyful experience, out of the normal time/space experience, that lets them travel to extraordinary, lost or fantastic places, or to different levels of reality.

Scientific objects

However, we are not here to tour, but to work. Thus, let's consider objects in the processes of scientific work. In fact, we are not totally detached from social science here, since those cultural-theme apparatuses have been built based on historic, archaeologic and anthropologic knowledge, if we are lucky. Think of any case you want, and you will find that contemporary professionals would be involved, at least through books, articles or other sources that inspire exhibits and architectures. Sometimes, scientific research is being conducted among the tourists who are traveling around; in several places, research processes are also part of the motifs in the display or the tourist package.

But that kind of work is also connected to other spaces and organized things. Libraries and archives are, for example, configurations of things within imposed hierarchies, classifications, and directions to inform the general public, but particularly students and scholars. We can say that in those places we are among dead people talking to each other through published or private documents. In materials from more contemporary times, we can recognize words, expressions, graphics and drawings. But as we go to older materials, the understanding can be difficult, and we need etymology, philology, paleography or even epigraphy. Reading transforms itself increasingly into a deeper experience of interpreting and deciphering. We also move from contemporary libraries to public archives, and then to special collections or to some restricted pieces of writing that are not available for public consultation. The use of replicas works well here, although the quality of facsimiles is always under discussion. All these approaches to the past comprehend different techniques and strategies, and serve to produce contemporary orders of the past, and end up in new hierarchies, time schemes, mappings, and cause-effect relationships, and in different effects of time/space ordering. The apex of the journey is our present time and place, the here and now, but the journeys eventually go far back or away, so we experience the same time/space travel effect. In other cases, because we need the information from living people, we begin a new process of documentation through ethnography, on paper or now increasingly through other forms or media. That documentation is going to be available for further research or public consultations, or even shown, eventually, in parks or museums, or stored in libraries and archives. The same happens with current research in natural science, which produces new knowledge, papers and audiovisual documentation; samples for labs, databases, images, and so on, that feed libraries, archives, and museums.

Objects produced in these overlapping and intermixed processes, which could be classified as the production of knowledge, could also be consumed in other areas of production. For example, scientific products are used in schools and universities to produce new scientific workers. Time-space travel devices and the ordering of chaos are very useful in schooling because they play an important part in technical and theoretical training. New scientists learn and then easily speak about geologic eras or historic epochs, areas of the globe, scales of time and space, and classifications and hierarchies of things and peoples. The whole learning process results in the production of basic metalanguages and standards in each discipline, while knowledge-transmission implies performing and stabilizing scientific practices. Another important effect is related to abstraction, since many areas of knowledge depend on concepts and principles that are part of logical thinking, as well as mathematics-like languages that could require a material support, a materialization. Schemas and diagrams can be useful in this sense, but abstractions can also be represented by (for instance) art-like displays, installations, and footage obtained via microscopes or telescopes, as well as by digital reconstructions. All these methods and apparatuses serve to materialize abstractions[12] and could function as an expected effect of framing.

We can say that effects such as ordering from chaos, time/space travel, metalanguages, standards and materialization of abstractions have been products of scientific work, and vice versa. And we scientists, as individuals, are just a tiny part of the wide and transcendent process. However, the process depicted here in an abstract way neither works in the same form everywhere nor follows linear trajectories and logics everywhere. On the contrary, framing implies areas or moments of misunderstandings, disputes and destabilization.

Discontinuities

Museums and the archive device serve to produce arrays of things. The resulting arrays can change in unanticipated ways under different pressures and expectations. Almost every museum and archive has its history of discontinuity and rupture. Here, I want to talk about the Náprstek museum of African, Asian and American Cultures, which was established during the 19th century in Prague, Czech Republic. The Museum has an interesting history of a discontinuous trajectory.

It was in 1862 when a Czech nationalist and modernist intellectual from Bohemia, then part of the Austrian Empire, started thinking about a museum of industry in Prague. Vojta Nápsrtek was a young Czech student in Vienna when the 1848 revolution broke out. Slavic nationalist groups in the Empire were asking for more administrative autonomy, but the central government rejected their demands and occupied the rebel areas, thus restoring its authority. In the following years, many Czechs and Slovaks ended up in the United States, as did Náprstek, although he did it for personal reasons. After 10 years in America, mainly in Milwaukee, Wisconsin, he returned home and started several projects with the financial help of his mother, a prosperous owner of a beer factory.

Náprstek promoted new household technologies, such as the telephone, electricity, and gas supply for kitchens; he also enrolled in a tourist club, which succeeded in having a tower built (the Petřín), which was inspired by the Eiffel Tower in Paris. Náprstek and his wife, Josefa, also started a library and a women's philosophical club, called the "American club" because it was supposed to be inspired by American liberal ideas. Conferences and workshops were given in public areas to spread new ideas and technologies. Among these activities, he proposed to build a museum of industry, motivated by his visit to the 1862 World Exhibition held in London. He himself was a member of the Bohemian delegation to the Exhibition. Therefore, he started collecting objects to be placed in the museum, to add to the machines and educational materials he had already brought from London[13].

Objects thus arrived from different parts of Europe and overseas, donated by Czech travelers and Czechs living abroad. The objects included some from Náprstek's personal collections, such as pieces that he had collected during his 1857 travels to the Lakes and Dakota Indian areas, which he had visited while living in Milwaukee, in the United States. Collections were proposed to show the different technologies, machines and instruments (mostly for domestic use) from all around the globe, ranging from the simplest ones to the most complex and sophisticated ones[14]. The first version of the Museum, which was opened to the public in the 1880s, consisted of cabinets in an expansion of his family's house. However, that space proved to be insufficient for displaying collections. A new building was needed. Time passed, as well as Náprstek life: he died in 1894, followed by his wife in 1907. The city then took charge of running the museum, at about the same time as the new Czechoslovakia was founded with the help of American Czechs and the American government in 1919 (at the end of World War I, and after the defeat of the Austrian Empire). Different policies during the following years arranged the archives, collections and museums in a new way, making them part of the European collections that ended up in other historical and technological museums in the city. The Náprstek museum kept the remaining objects and, because of the character of those collections, it was transformed into the Museum of General Ethnography. Afterwards, during the German occupation, the museum changed again, to become part of the National Museum. Shortly afterward, another rearrangement of objects occurred, with new classifications such as European or overseas, technology or arts, Slavic objects, etc. After World War II, the museum was included in the National Museum system, and in 1962, it got its present name, based on its remaining collections: the Náprstek Museum of

Asian, African and American Cultures (Náprstkovo muzeum asijských, afrických a amerických kultur)[15].

The history of Náprstek museum shows how the same device (museum/archive) has been used for two different, and in some ways opposing, purposes. From being a place to celebrate civilization, industry and technology (with all its consequences) and materializing the meaning of civilization, time/space hierarchies and standardization by comparing and classifying different tools and instruments, the Náprstek museum everywhere turned into one dedicated to overseas cultures. Today it resembles the form of other anthropological museums that arrange objects by areas and then by special qualities.

Authenticity and reliability

Even though Náprstek originally designed and directed the museum as an important part of his efforts to promote technology and civilization, it was then transformed into a museum about non-European cultures. That is why it includes pieces of interest for Mexicans like me. There is, for example, an unauthentic or falsified Maya codex, called the Liberec or Prague Codex. An analysis performed in the 1950s declared it a falsified document, a fake codex, made and sold in the 19th century. However, it is now conjectured—and disputed—that beneath the falsified drawings lies a hidden authentic part, which could be revealed by using current photographic technologies[16]. This case exemplifies another area of dispute: authenticity.

The relation between arts and sciences in the case of anthropology and history is clearer when considering the specific, political conditions of building nations and ethnicities. Contrary to the arguments of most nationalists and ethnicists, the very existence of nations and ethnic groups over long periods of time is problematic. The idea of nations or ethnic groups seems to be an epistemological device, a specific variety of those devices that forms order from chaos, time/space arrays and connections, and frames to stabilize relationships. Sometimes, it is not strange that narratives about nations and ethnic groups were produced by archaeological sites, historical towns, and the raising or remodeling of museums, as well as by archives and libraries[17]. It is not strange, either, that ideas of nations and ethnic groups, which could have been classified as abstractions in some way, are spread through public arts to reach the wider audience, as in the case of post-revolutionary Mexican muralism, paintings and music.

After the Mexican revolution (1910-1917), some artists started an aesthetic movement in search of the authentic Mexicanhood, supposedly residing within the people and their traditions, colors and movements. Muralism, a form of art expressed in pieces painted on huge walls open to audiences, occupied public buildings to create Mexicanhood, recreating popular scenes, historic motives and personages, as well as exalting the revolutionary classes and leaders (probably influenced by the Russian Revolution). The history of Mexican anthropology is also clearly connected to this political and aesthetic movement, whereas some motifs in the paintings were inspired by archaeological excavations, like the pyramids. The Mexican soul itself, as an aesthetic, political and intellectual concept, was materialized by painters and anthropologists of the time[18]. After five decades, a stable concept of Mexican aesthetics was then exported, sometimes influencing other spheres, as happened through the first exhibits of Mexican art and culture in Japan, studied by Sukikara[19].

Scientific knowledge can thus transcend the field of science and be transformed into political or aesthetic devices, with their expected effect. If we don't have a nation, we can use these techniques to materialize a nation as we had materialized other type of abstractions. It is not uncommon that artists remake scientific objects in aesthetic forms, as has happened in literature, painting, sculpture and film production (like in the Sun Tower in Osaka). Today, we can find diverse examples of this in science-fiction literature or in popular art paintings in museums. It is said, for example, that Mel Gibson, in making his film Apocalypto, took the advice of anthropologists. The film projected a highly stratified pre-Columbian Maya society, where elites performed human sacrifices on the top of pyramids, in front of a crowded square. The social divisions also included the people living at the edges of the spectacle, although they would be obligated by force to be part of it—a very central part of it in fact. That social edge, which was about to be integrated in the sacrificial center, was the point of departure of the film. However, the film caused a great annoyance among some anthropologists living in Chiapas. Discussions revolved around publicity and the film's historical accuracy, as well as around the anthropology that informed the film maker. As we get passionately involved within these discussions, we also participate in the effect of authenticity.

Framing and political epistemology

We probably know that the intended effects of displays are not always realized or totally accomplished; that incomplete, momentary views of displays through the windows of cars and airliners can cause the intended effect to collapse, thus giving an experience of anachronism or a feeling of unauthenticity. So can conversations between surrounding visitors, locals or employees. However, to confront those feelings and understandings we keep making better museums, archaeological sites and historical villages, as well as festivals and fairs with people dressing in historical costumes, and with artefacts, foods, beverages, technologies, music, dances and plays that represents otherness in space and time. Maybe it is because of their effects. That is why these devices are found world-wide, because they produce time/space experiences, order, standards, metalanguages, materiality, authenticity and realism. All these effects conform the way in which we organize our experiences of things when we are touring for educational, scientific or recreational reasons.

The history of these devices is closely related to other parts of the contemporary world, going back 200 to 300 years. The cabinets of curiosities and personal collections and libraries, including different deposits of old documents, precede the devices and effects that appeared afterwards. Their histories could tell us many things about the ways we stabilize and organize materiality in our time. They can be analyzed as frames, in terms of Miller or Grosz. Miller says that materiality does not refer to objects by themselves, but to the way they are organized to create frames for action and understandings[20]. Grosz, from a very different perspective, analyzes how our sense of the world (our nervous system) is deeply influenced and mutually transformed by the ways we frame objects, taking glimpses of them from chaos, like the artist that frames certain things to extract and sustain sensations[21]. Museums, theme parks, archaeological sites and archives are all part of the way we frame selected objects, and mostly our experiences of those objects. Studying the effects of framing involved in those devices, and their inner claims to stability, authenticity and realism, could reveal parts of our present epistemology; that is, our experience of reality and materiality. It could even show us different kinds of political (or metapolitical) work, which has materialized the frames that order and stabilize the basic metalanguage and standardized forms of scientific objects, and also transforms the ways in which we frame objects, and our experience of them.

That's all. Thank you very much.

Inoue: Thank you, thank you so much for your presentation. You gave us how materials are kept, reserved, interconnected, spread with the technology and higher class skill within time and space; how the framing functions as the device of selecting materials. So please give us your comment, Professor Gatta.

Gianluca Gatta
Migration and Archive
Gianluca Gatta: Thanks to Professer Ogasawara and the other organizers for inviting me to discuss this thought-provoking paper, which I found not only interesting in itself, as a good attempt to generalize some aspects of the relationship between knowledge, power and materiality, but also because it resonates with my research experience with objects. Since Professer Escalona Victoria's empirical referents are quite different from mine, I think there is room for a fruitful comparison. Briefly, my experience with objects is related to border-crossing migrants' objects found in a dump, i.e. lost objects, seized objects, forcibly separated from the owners. They are present objects, not objects related

to the past. I think that this first difference would allow us to take into account the temporal dimension of the relationship between objects and owners. As I was saying, I'm very interested in reflecting on this construction of a more general theory of the object-knowledge relationship, contrasting it with very different ethnographic settings.

I would like to start my comment from the end: framing. I am convinced by your analysis of the interaction between politics, scientific knowledge, and art, as not totally separate domains of social life, but as spheres that intertwine in our everyday lives, as scholars, activists, and common citizens. If my understanding is correct, you think that every act of knowledge about objects, as abstraction, has a sort of stabilizing effect. So, objects distanced from chaos need some stabilizing, more abstract concepts to frame them, to organise them. And, in this process, abstract knowledge needs to be materialized through, for instance, boring graphs or more interesting pieces of art. And I agree on this point. So, interaction between knowledge and materialization of concepts is a key issue. It is a kind of solidification, a sort of 'freezing' of the objects' meaning, of the meaning of what our ideas transfer to objects. It is also a way to overcome the limits of verbal language, as it happens with body language and nonverbal communication in general, I think. And so, through the analysis of frames we can discover how we stabilize and organize materiality.

My first question: if this analysis of frames is a sort of demystifying or disclosing process, can we add a sort of new layer of reflexivity to it? To what objects is this analysis related? What kinds of stabilization does the analysis of frame itself produce? Is it a way to restore chaos from a type of order that we perceive as problematic, such as the one established through concepts of nation, ethnicization, and racialization? Or, is it a way to try constructing new orders in the frame of political epistemology? You do not talk about epistemology in general but about "political epistemology", namely, reflecting on how to know what is a just world. So, to sum up, what is the relationship between the reflexive self-awareness of the process that you have analysed and the chaos-order of materiality?

A second issue concerns with Náprstek museum. You say that "the same device, museum/archive, has been used for two different, and in some ways opposed, purposes". I would like to better understand what you mean for "in some ways", especially in the light of the fact that, as a kind of materialization of anthropological ideas, this museum's history seems to reflect the history of modern anthropology and culture theories, namely, the passage from evolutionary paradigm to historical particularism. Since it became a museum of other cultures, as you have said, I would like to know more about the biographical life of these objects, and particularly what happened to the European objects in this shift.

And a couple of other comments: One concerns hierarchies. You mentioned libraries, archives and, of course, for the purposes of time, you mentioned all these devices together. But there are many differences, some of them are more hierarchical, some of them less. I think that it would be interesting to reflect on the relationship between material archives and digital archives, characterized by, maybe only in appearance, non-hierarchical forms of knowledge organization and archiving. Digital archives are not based on a stable hierarchical structure of layers, but are dynamic and user-oriented, even if they are not as "anarchist" as they appear, because there is a "hidden and non-accessible programmatic organization that also characterises the search engines used when surfing the net"[22]. So, how are these technological innovations affecting the construction of hierarchies in the relationship between immaterial and material?

About authenticity, I was very shocked to discover that in Wikipedia there is a page named "the culture of Mexico". I found it in "the history of Mexico". It was quite interesting to notice that, even if the content is historical and complex – the page talks about the muralist, the revolution, etc. – the label "the culture of Mexico" reproduces a framing that draws on a very old-fashioned approach to culture. I would like to know your opinion about this dissonance.

Another point concerns the effects of devices. You analyzed how museums – especially natural and archaeological museums – produce order and time-space travel effects. You said that we "enjoy these staged experiences of time-space oscillation, and use them to get out of everyday life and chores" and we "travel fantastic, unlocated places". The issue of "separation from everyday life" is a dominant trope in social sciences and I was wondering how it can be connected to a theory of the sacred; but not in terms of Durkheim's religious sociology, according to which: "sacred things are simply collective ideals that have fixed themselves on material objects"[23] that have been separated from everyday life. Here, I am thinking about a theory of the sacred developed by Ernesto de Martino, one of the founding fathers of Italian anthropology. His theory is focused on more "technical" functions of the sacred and conceives mythology and rituals as "tools" employed to "dehistoricize" the human beings' experience, in order to return to history in case of crisis. They are a "technique – or system of techniques – for facing the risk of alienation and re-disclosing those formal powers which crisis threatens to paralyze"[24]. Central in de Martino's theory is the concept "crisis of presence"[25], experienced by individuals in the face of harsh material conditions of life, for instance peasants overcome by continuous pregnancies, etc. So, rituals are not transcendent things but are settled in everyday life and allow individuals to overcome what he calls the "anguish at history which does not repeat itself"[26], just temporarily entering a fantastic space out of history, not to escape but just to restore their "presence" in society. It's a sort of therapeutic aspect of mythical-ritual apparatuses rooted in the concrete and socially stratified existential precariousness[27].

I am wondering if it might be useful to understand these contemporary forms of "traveling out of history" in terms of crisis of and restoration to "presence". I am aware that using the concepts of religion and the sacred to understand the contemporary world is controversial, but from this point of view it could be quite interesting. Perhaps the analysis of this kind of anguish produced by history could also be applied, reflexively, to our everyday life as researchers, in dealing with our objects, but also with news. Sometimes we look for this new "space" in order to temporarily distancing ourselves from interpretive crisis and from the perception of the abyss between our disciplinary common sense and news. For example, the other day, the right-wing mayor of a small Italian town said that school trips to Auschwitz are not good because they are politically biased, partisan. So, how do we deal with distressing news like this? How do we overcome the burden of these kinds of processes affecting our research and lives? What strategies do we adopt, as researchers, to escape from and restore our "presence-in-the-world"? And, how do we discern this kind of "healing" temporary travel out of history from an escape without return? I am very sensitive to this, because I have been working on migrants' border crossing and, sometimes, I need to explore other objects of thought to temporarily escape this kind of epistemological and psychological burden. I produced chaos. It is up to you now to stabilize what I said, if it makes sense for you. Thank you very much.

Inoue: Thank you, Professor Gatta. You pronounced our perspective when you thought about the paper. So I think you have though about your thinkings to do so.

Q&A

José Luis: Thank you very much for the very nice questions. I love this discussion, and I think we share the same concerns. Firstly, it's interesting because I think that this is probably one of the most important points in doing social sciences: how do we materialize knowledge and, at the same time, how do we create historical and political frames? Or, how have the objects that we are working with—and we ourselves, in an extreme view of the process of making social science—been produced by social sciences? I see the social sciences as a bunch of devices that probably produce authenticity, reliability, stabilization, and reality. I don't like all of the parts and consequences of this process very much, but this is what really exists in social science. And many social scientists do this because they get money. We collaborate in the construction of the world by doing this. It's difficult to find someone who gets money to destroy this world, for example. It's quite difficult. But, at the same time, in this productive sense,

I mean, we are also destroying the world, anyway. But how can we think about and remodel our frames? That is the question. I think that this is a very important issue because it means to figure out new forms of progressive sciences; because we understand we are made scientists as well as, at the same time, we do science. And, if we make our frames visible from a historical perspective, we can also change those frames. We can change or engage in another frame. And this is not only our frame, but the frame that orders things around us, like in museums or schools, understood as ordering devices. I think that's my main point, this is the reason for me to call this perspective a political epistemology. We are touching the very ways we are making this world, and the very ways the world is making us. That's important.

And we have two ways to do so: we are some kind of Marxists, or radical social scientists who work to transform this world; or we have a radical anarchist position and want to make chaos, probably as you suggested. These are two different ways to escape from framing, to transform the world, transform the scientific knowledge, arts and the social world, and transcend the immediate worries and struggles confined within the frames unnoticed.

And yes, you are right in saying that it is reflexivity. This is very short paper, one that has to do with some aspects of this broader movement of knowledge, science and devices. I am just noticing how important it is to work on frames, because they affect our way of deciding what is stable and what is not; what is readable, and what is not; what is in the right scale, and what is not. That is the discussion. That is a very interesting point because in every "making" process in art or science, as in the making of a film, the maker chooses which tone or which music fits best to produce a particular emotion, meaning or effect upon the public, in a wider sense. And it's very difficult because, in western standardized music for example, we have only twelve tones in one scale, and we make a lot of different types of music with them. So, stabilization is clearly a very interesting process that affects in many ways the forms in which we perceive and feel reality. I understand this stabilization as one way to start defining the concept of materiality. And we need the kind of reflexivity that I am talking about to see the living interweaving and overlapping in the making of sciences, publics, and scientists, by pointing to shared frames.

Probably this is my point, and probably you catch me subsumed unknowingly in my own hierarchy of problems, you know. For example, and as you told me, when I summarized the history of the Náprstek museum as a form of opposition, between celebration of industrialization and progress and celebration of multi-culturality, as a reflexion of the progress of anthropologic knowledge. Yes, probably you are right. I was wrong in making this division between celebrations of civilization and celebration of multi-culturality. Probably this is not a clear sample of breaking of frames in knowledge and devices, but a continuity or a parallel development, yes, it's right. I must change that impression in my paper.

Gatta: Or probably not. Because in anthropology there was a sort of paradigmatic shift. So, it is quite right.

José Luis: Yes, but I think that I need to think through the issue of changes in anthropologic thinking from 19th century to 20th centuries, and in contemporary discussions. Yes, I just need to say this: I will adopt your position because the Museum in the Czech Republic displays a hierarchy, like many others of its type. And, also, it belongs to a national order of archives and memoires: there was also the foundation of a museum of technology. So, the collections were allocated to those places under a clear logic. The rest, which did not belong to those classifications (Slavic or Czech History, European culture, industry and technology, etc.) were placed in a museum for ethnology or anthropology. It is not an isolated and specific case. Instead, it resembled wider classifications, hierarchizations and orders of things in the relationship between some institutions in North Atlantic empires, nations and democracies and the rest of the world. So, yes, you're right. I must explore more cases and look for details about what could be, certainly, a more problematic and discontinuous history in the Náprstek museum.

You're right also about another point. Framing is used to make and to employ technology to produce materiality (which represents complex relations between humans and things), but we could work and think in more-democratic forms to classify and stabilize knowledge. Yes, it is a logical consequence of my argument. We now have technologies that can be used to transcend the established hierarchies and orders. We anthropologists started by taking some things like the representation or materialization of culture; we even produced special words (like "culture"), and classifications that made us gather and enclose particular things. Then, we constructed buildings, which have been transformed for new things and novel ways to collect, deposit and exhibit those things. We started schooling young people to be new specialists in different parts of the process. But now we have new technologies, and these electronic devices could affect our ways of materializing knowledge. I think this is a very interesting field to explore: how we re-build the world with more-democratic devices like TIC. But now we must question whether those new devices could produce a more democratic knowledge-making process.

The kinds of effects that are not connected to science, but to "inmateriality", are another important area of exploration[28]. Yes, you're right. I want to think about churches, temples or other places that have been used for similar purposes, to produce another sensation, another form of ordering things and hierarchies. This is probably a much more important question because ideas of god, animism, church, religion, and sacred things are more extended among people all over the world: more so than science, and for a much longer time, too. And it is possible that there could be some kinds of connections between those buildings that materialize the unmaterial, between temples and museums (that have been established for new sacred inmaterialities like nations, ethnicities and progress). I don't know how to answer this question right away. And yes, it's all about effects. But at the same time, we could explore such issues with a perspective on frames. This is just an invitation, you know; an invitation to think of frames: how we historically frame things and allocate things to positions within frames, and how we can change our ways of doing so by confronting the subject of framings itself. Thank you for the very interesting and enlightening questions.

Gatta: What you said is interesting, and the paper made me reflect more, I found many possible connections, and this is productive. It confirms its heuristic power. I would like to add some comments about what you said regarding two possible approaches to overcome more essentialist forms of objectivation. With a hint of irony, I propose to call the two approaches that you mentioned, "Leninist" approach and "Anarchist" approach. "Anarchists" aim to produces chaos, they do not need to relate to materiality. Maybe they do not need abstractions, or they just want to destroy them. But, if reflexive researchers or cultural activists are more attracted by the other approach, the "Leninist", what kind of objects should they opt for? What kind of materialized abstractions can we produce in light of this analysis of frames? It is quite hard to think about how we can do it. Maybe art can pursue this goal. How can art translate this need for self-understanding of our frames? Of course, art is always in the future, so maybe it already does it and we need to explore art and suggest new ways to materialize it. Thank you.

Inoue: So we have a proceeding to questions about session. Please let the session more chaotic with your words. Why you can't stop to stabilize. 日本語でも。

Public 1: Thank you for the interesting presentation Professor José Luis. I'm so interested in discussing in global scale about this materialism of archives, because this talk actually reminds me of the talk from, I forgot the name, but a professor of anthropology from the university of British Colombia, Canada. She came to Kobe and she gave a talk about changes of exhibition of contemporary in Canada. It took place at an art gallery in Vancouver. And she pointed out that there was this change; the art gallery originally didn't really represent the indigenous tribe, and then like in this piece they install to show more of them being an indigenous tribe. I concentrate to what you call like that, this spending time in crossover when the phenomenon like populism and cosmopolitanism in this globalization world like borders of the countries like dimensions, and like some voices I'm so worried about our culture diminishing if we keep it open and represent some cultural "affect". So we have to make someone have the limit of affect. I always question about what is culture anyway. So when you want to preserve or fix the culture, you need this kind of materialism. And, now I forgot my question. So you know, in this global scale, like Professor Gatta said, the linguistic has its own limit to express something. And somehow more non-linguistic language is more available to our communication when we want to express our ideology or when we want to construct some identities. We need some figures or other non-linguistic expressions.

Let me arrange my words. Ok, it also connects to power and knowledge because in my word, in short to say, because power and knowledge, it's like two points which produce each other. So in this global scale, not only in this world including Mexico, how social anthropologists see this, this materialism of archive and also its fabrication, because we know that will be like many fabrications when you want to construct something by materializing our idea. How to see this in this global scale when we see there are two of both in every country. For example, in the talk from the professor from the University of British Columbia I could see this is a change when they try to make it more tribal. I could see that and they want to force the multicultural image. Because in this populism era or in this time globalization era we know that Canada has this image of the most multicultural stage like something. So I could see that we have to keep the image going. Like if you know Japan, Kyoto, they have some really cosmetic multiculturalism and wants to show that this is the Japan; we keep tradition materiality. So that kind of materialism wants to leave in force there in the image. So how do you think this in this global scale? Thank you.

José Luis: This is the big question. I think that we, in some way, are trapped in the kind of materialism that we produce. We know that words like nations, states and ethnicities, or cultural as well as racial groups, can be viewed from different perspectives, and that they belong in part to the materialism we inherited. That is a "natural division", so to say; "natural" because this is controlled by the prevalent order of materialism, and was stabilized in long historical processes, using devices like those I mentioned in my presentation. So, we have a lot to do with frames, which somehow enables us to dematerialize those nation-narratives, ethno-narratives, and so on. And, of course, this is a global issue, you're right. We normally think that such things are located in places, areas or points, separately, each one with its particular past; but as we approach the locality of those social products, we also see that some critical objects and processes are not entirely local. They are local in some ways, but not totally local, even if there initially existed some kind of locality, of particularity. And we should be aware of that, at least in doing ethnography. At the same time, we need to formulate an alternative type of problematization. I mean, we know the right way to problematize in anthropology, naturally, because we start planning our exploration from views already built up; for instance, from racial, ethnic or national frames. That's why we need to explore frames most seriously. I think so, because that issue also concerns (as one example of a different perspective, a different view) questions of cosmopolitanism in localities[29]. We do not start with the question of what is specific here, but from what has been specifically produced there in connection, disconnection or transposition to other there's and here's. It probably does not make much sense to talk about cosmopolitanism here, in Kobe, because things here seem to be potentially and factually global in different ways than those in which I have been doing ethnography. It is different in Chiapas, where I live, because it is very far away from everything. But even there we can see and feel the historical dislocation of things, animals, plants, ideas and people. But here you can sense that, you can see the flux of the world in different ways, even in intimacy, faster than we in Chiapas in some respects. Locality in this sense, from a different frame, leads us into a very different bunch of questions. I could talk of alternative devices in contrast to localist frames[30]. We can also use or construct other words to name things, so we explore new meta-languages. Art is very important in that area because making a new meta-language can serve in the same way that artefacts and art do: to realize, to reach and extract sensations, new senses of this world or new orders from chaos. I don't know if I am making the point in the right way, but you're right in posing this question. It is another interesting and enlightening area for a perspective on framing.

Public 1: Because I know the knowledge is politicized also.

José Luis: Yes. Probably the first step in doing social science and doing art is to politicize, by asking questions, and probably the most radical questions emerge as we problematize frames (instead of continuing to move within the established frames) [31]. That's the invitation.

Public 2: Those things to develop, I mean, in some questions. First of all, José Luis, you gave us a really kind of paradigm changing perspective to us about things. Sometime, including students, including ourselves, we talked about the abstract, theoretical things; people ask you, give me materials, give me evidence, you know you have to prove, concrete examples then we can bring in something like "this is a material, this is the proof". But listening to your talk, it's opposite, I mean, a certain thing can be really abstract, can be really just a representation of something happening in the past. So we have to clear up my mind, our mind once again, because even if you brought some concrete things it doesn't necessary mean that you display concrete evidence. It's important, isn't it?

Another thing. I have been to Hokkaido the other day, and we visited Ainu kotan. Maybe Ayami will display something later. Next year, in time of Tokyo Olympics for some reasons, I don't know, they will be a very big Ainu cultural museum called Upopoi（民族共生象徴空間）, National Ainu Museum. Everything around form Ainu villages; old one, new one or contemporary one will be displayed. We went to a meeting with an Ainu association. And some of them really didn't like this idea, because once you are ordering stuffs, they are contained in certain spaces, displayed as a cultural item. One of those said "it stocks our history". We stock our history. Still with discrimination, I guess, the Ainu people, indigenous population in Hokkaido, in marriage and employment; how is the discrimination in everything, the social status is not equal. But our lives are going to be culturalized as something to be preserved in certain spaces, which is heavily funded by the Japanese government because the government don't want to enthuse they are; they have enthused, their indigenous population but there is no compensation or reconciliation. So in social and political contexts they are still striving but in cultural context their culture is a kind of frozen in certain spaces, in the co-habitation space. That is bad. That's why you have to quote from politicization of art or politicization of aesthetic. Well maybe it can be expanding in global scale, not only for certain ethnicities or tribes, but also I think it is happening everywhere, now. You say something? Chaotic questions?

Public 3: With regard to the framing you talked about, I think it may also relate to the language. The language works as frame in some way, and I would like to discuss more about such question. I will comment about it in the final session but it also will be good to talk now about it, making chaos. For example, the word of Maya. When we use this term, we would bring to mind various ideas related to it: civilization, people who are good at the numbers, or mysterious space etc.. It means, I guess, the word can be a storage; it is the storage of the meanings which have accumulated in itself and at the same time the word can be a device which takes meanings out.

　日本語でいいですか。framing の話で、言語が framing する。言語によって framing されるスペースもあるし、時間空間的な問題もあるし、そこをもうちょっとわたしは掘り下げたいなと思っていて、コメントは後でそれをしようかなと思ってたんですけど、もし今そういう話が出来ればと思ってちょっとカオスを混じらせたんですが。例えば、Maya っていう言葉、そういう term を使っ

た時にもうわたしたちは多分いろんな ideas が出てくる。文明であったり、数
字に強い人たちとか、ミステリアスな空間とか。その言葉自体がもう倉庫で
あるし、過去に形成されてきた言葉に積み重なってきた意味の倉庫でもあるし、
それをはきだしていく device でもあると思う。言葉自体が。

Public 4: In this morning session, I think we framed; this space looks like a chaos
but I think, really we have to bring back the chaotic state to the order of things
fixed in the museums or any other public spaces. Because things essentially are
open to interpretation, the meaning, power and memories always contested in
things. And they might lead to multiple understanding, multiple intent to resist in
fixed ideas placed up on it, but in a kind of meeting museum representations like
one that Hiroki mentioned about exhibition, possibly the vision of this cultural
museum of Ainu in Hokkaido. I mean the meaning, this kind of fixation is going
because they want to tell and bring in certain messages and statements inscribed
in those things, even so they may have other memories as a power inside, so
people who used to own project feel ambivalent about it. So, into the situation of
Canada and Australia, this is more the museum than art galleries and ethnographic
museums. That is chaotic by now because from the objects as seen as fine art. A
lot of exhibition arts faced with ironical prices of art market, so it's fine to say,
to tell them that this is an art. But you can pay for those or just basket or use
whatever, so some people still feel actions or feel offended to see all these very
primitive materials situated in the centre of the art gallery next to some very quite
famous paintings, whatever. But in reality we are mixing all of the boundaries and
meanings or webs in those spaces. So the public have to go back to chaotic state,
to be informed in the order of whole things.

José Luis: I think this is also a really interesting issue: why not go back to chaos?
I think this is what some colleagues call anthropologic anarchism, inspired by
Deleuze and Guattari, of course. Elizabeth Grosz, for example, goes to see chaos,
in order to understand how deeply artificial our understanding of the world is,

and what we scientists miss in terms of sensation. That is to say, of that which emerges from the connections between our nervous system and the vibrant forces of the universe, far beyond our human experience —an experience that constitutes a highly conceptualized framing (framed in scientific way, by coordinates and scales, I dare to say). That's basically a philosophical and conceptual position for our thinking in social sciences, particularly since we work inside frames. And, also, it is not an issue for scientists, exclusively. We appreciate, we see things in museums or in villages, and our experience is quite stable in different ways. Differences appear because we are not the same people; we are not the same readers, the same travellers, the same observers of a particular object. Each of us can and may understand different things. But we can never really foresee the effects of those understandings. We need to explore that. What kind of effects can a museum of things that are not quiet produce, a museum of moving things or moving characters? What effect could a museum produce if exhibits didn't emphasize one place or one identity, but instead showed that we don't have identity, that we have movement, that we are becoming, that we change? Why do we keep making museums of culture and identity in the old-fashioned style, framed by stabilized ideas of culture/place/people confined within a fixed location and time? That's the question. And I think it's a call for all of us to be more creative, and to face chaos firstly, to go to the basis and to return with alternative views and frames. I think this is (I'm probably currently reading too much of Deleuze and Guattari) the way to transcribe important questions in anthropology of frames, the question I am concerned with nowadays. There is also another issue. We know that museums are not the same devices forever; museums change, just as churches and every building has, and the way every device we construct is doing right now. Everything is melting as new things solidify once and again. This is the Marxist view of "culture" in capitalism, as David Harvey reminded us. We need to remember that we developed those different forms of materiality. That is, forms that differ from the capitalist way of producing produce materiality, which produces commodities as well as values animated or haunted by other forms of value. We need to remember, too, that we are still learning how those mechanism or devices are working out in everyday life, and probably the ways that frames intervene in the production and destruction of those things and our experience and sensation of materiality today.

Gatta: I think that some issues of our debate could be enriched by a reflection on the "new spirit of capitalism"[32], and particularly its adoption of horizontality instead of hierarchization. We referred to the possibility of developing democratic ways of archiving. And horizontality instead of hierarchization seems to be a basic precondition. But, is it enough to be truly democratic? I work with participatory methods in migrants' self-representation, so I am part of this anti-hierarchical approach that tries to explore chaos and destroy fixed identities and classification, but I am wondering if this shifting in frame can be captured by power as well. Maybe, one way to explore it is to include the concept intersectionality in the discussion about identity and materiality, saying every time basic things like: "Ok, you're identifying yourself with this object but you are not only Ainu". It is a way to explore the hiding and materializing effects of identities border constructions.

About the participatory approaches, I would like to share a personal story. As I was mentioning before, I am part of an association, the Archive of migrant memories[33], that works on "participatory video" projects involving migrants. So, its core activity is self-narration, starting from concrete biographical experiences, which is something completely different from top-down "community identification". Some years ago, my association was involved in the first steps of a project by an institutional museum in Rome. It was a former ethnographic museum, full of objects. Today, there is a heated debate about the meaning of that kind of museum[34]; they are considered to be containers of useless old staff, totally detached from the present or, quite the opposite, as something that should be re-semantized in order to have a new active and critical role in the present, but how? The line of reasoning of the project promoters was as follows: "We cannot reproduce the colonial hierarchy, we have postcolonial migrants in Rome, what can we do with the museum's objects by involving migrants?". So, they got in touch with us in order to implement the project. For our part, we proposed to organize, following our participatory approach and in a more "chaotic" and critical way – a series of workshops with migrants. The aim was to let migrants be inspired by the objects in producing their own self-narration, putting the objects at the service of migrants and not the migrants at the service of the museum. Our proposal was accepted, but we were asked not to select "common" migrants – as in our previous activities – but people holding leadership in their communities. That institutional logic – "why did you select Ahmed from Morocco, instead of the leader of the Moroccan community?" – risked taking for granted and reinforcing power relations inside the national/ethnic communities of migrants, and for this reason we refused this hierarchical approach and the collaboration came to an abrupt halt. For us, that approach was just reproducing community identification, reframing those objects through established power relations.

The last point concerns "silence", which you mentioned before. Recently, I have been invited to reflect on my research through the lenses of the anthropology of silence, and I found that silence has a strict relationship with objects and materiality. Moreover, silence also can play a fundamental role in the trans-generational transmission of experience. There is interesting research by anthropologist Carol Kidron about memory transmission of the Auschwitz survivors to their children in Israel, through silence[35]: not politicized and verbalized memories, not claimed identity as survivors, but hidden memories transmitted through objects and silent interaction and reconstructed as adults by their children. Among Kidron's ethnographic descriptions, there is a story of a spoon, the spoon that the mother of an interviewee used in Auschwitz. After the liberation, that spoon did not become a relic, but was used daily in that family to feed their children:

"This was my mother's spoon in Auschwitz. This is what she ate with, you know, the soup."

Attempting to restore my professional composure despite my surprise, I asked her where the spoon was kept in her parent's home, thinking that it must have been in some closed cabinet for safekeeping. She explained with a broader smile, "It was in the kitchen, in the drawer, with the other utensils... We ate with it. My mother fed me my morning oatmeal with it." At this point I was shocked. The phenomenology of the spoon from Auschwitz strikingly echoes the literature on material culture in everyday life.[36]

In such cases, the uses of objects pre-exist their new meanings, which arise only when the children collect information about the historical events in which their loved ones' stories were embedded, and also when the researchers ask them to talk about the transmission of memory. So, I think that this approach encourages us to include the affective aspects of the relationship with objects in our analysis. We can always deconstruct identity, but we should also keep in mind that in everyday life a sort of protection from chaos is needed by people and it also depends on the daily intersection between memories and objects.

Inoue: So it's time for closing. How are you ready to comment or questions? You have already enjoyed the session? Ok. So for me, I'm a political scientist and the political science has priority on evidence. That is fixed science, scientific and is always already providing devices. Today so you give us the world of object, that is the ingress to the chaos with many attractiveness. So in this sense you gave us another perspective against evidence; that is, the science is very dominant in all research fields. Thank you so much. Everybody, thank you.

Kayanoki: Thank you very much. So we are now having lunchtime. We restart at 1:45, so we have almost one and half hour.

1 "The wealth of societies in which the capitalist mode of production prevails appears as an "immense collection of commodities"; the individual commodity appears as its elementary form." Marx, Karl, *Capital, Volume 1*, Penguin Classics, 1976 [1867], pp. 125.

2 I am referring to the notion of framing as I took it from two different sources: Miller, Daniel 2005, "Materiality, An Introduction" in *Materiality*, Duke University Press, pp. 1-50; and Grosz, Elizabeth, 2008, *Chaos, Territory, Art*, Columbia University Press. I will explain differences in the following notes.

3 For experience I want to point to effects that emerge or are being triggered by certain type of relationships between subjects and objects, as constrained within artificiated frames, or human organized connections. It means that I am going to address experience as the expected influence of framed interactions among people and things, embracing either effects upon and within subjects as well as failure or unaccomplishment. I am referring here particularly to space-time, standardization, stability, realism, authenticity, and otherness, besides other effects, as compounds of coordinates of materiality (and immateriality).

4 For sensation, otherwise, I am referring to compounds of percepts and affects, that are mediated by materials, by different forms of materiality in arts, from architecture and painting to dynamic arts like music and dance. Inspired by Deleuze and Guattari, Elizabeth Grosz's analysis (op. cit.) of frames approaches the idea of planes of composition, an architecture that made possible the extraction of sensation in between our nervous system and chaos, the vibrant forces of the universe. Sensation upsurges by basic tensions, pre-verbalized and pre-conceptualized ways of being part of the chaos. Art is thus a compound of percepts and affects, a pure sensation materialized through objects, movements or sounds, that made possible the apparition of objects and subjects at the same time. My point here is that by referring to experience and sensation, I am inquiring into the possibility that both could occur in a single event as a confrontation between order and chaos (particularly in museums, archeological sites, archives or exotic villages, since these are not just scientific products but materialization of our uneven and long-lasting exploration inside chaos). See, also, Deleuze, Gilles and Félix Guattari, *What is Philosophy?* Columbia University Press, 1994.

5 The Tower of the Sun Museum, located at the Expo 70 Commemorative Park at Osaka, Japan, is particularly fine example of this evocation, since it is an apparatus/art object, a mixture of art and science, that displays pieces of artifacts to show the evolution of life and also an art-like-collection that is looking forward to explore the energies of all things in the universe, as it is said in the site webpage: https://taiyounotou-expo70.jp/en/about/ (28/09/2020).

6 The Tower of the Sun Museum, located at the Expo 70 Commemorative Park at Osaka, Japan, is particularly fine example of this evocation, since it is an apparatus/art object, a mixture

of art and science, that displays pieces of artifacts to show the evolution of life and also an art-like-collection that is looking forward to explore the energies of all things in the universe, as it is said in the site webpage: https://taiyounotou-expo70.jp/en/about/ (28/09/2020).

7 For information of the Digital Museum, see ILAM 2016, "Museo Digital, la gran propuesta de Copán Ruinas", Avialable at: https://ilam.org/index.php/noticias/novedades-del-patrimonio/item/1006-museo-digital-la-gran-propuesta-de-copan-ruinas (28/09/2020). For Harvard Scanning Project, see Barbara Fash and Alexandre Tokovinine, "3D Scanning Project, Peabody Museum's Corpus of Maya Hieroglyphic Inscriptions program (CMHI)", 2013, Available at: https://www.peabody.harvard.edu/node/821 (28/09/2020).

8 About the effect of othering: Fabian, Johannes, op. cit. In the context of making ethnography in Mexico, see also López, Paula "The effect of othering, The historical dialectic of local and national identity among the orignarios, 1950–2000", Anthropological Theory, Vol 9(2) 2009: 171–187; López, Paula and Ariadna Acevedo-Rodrigo (edits.), *Beyond Alterity, Destabilizing the Indigenous Other in Mexico*, 2018.

9 This visit reminded me the very popular visit to the Church in Chamula, Chiapas, México, where, after having paid for a ticket in the tourism municipal office, tourist can walk in between the worshipers, who are performing curings and offerings right there. Overwrapping logics and uses of places and things point to the implicit tensions and disputes in the realization of materiality. It is possible, in some cases, that tension materialize in political confrontation, as in the dispute between a mining company, scientists and shamans using a sacred area in northern Mexico (see, Liffman, Paul, "Historias, cronotopos y geografías wixaritari", *Relaciones Estudios de Historia y Sociedad*, [S.l.], v. 39, n. 156, nov. 2018. ISSN 2448-7554).

10 Song, Baleun, *Escenificar la cultura: mercantilización, turismo y estrategias de familias de Zinacantan, Chiapas*, Master Thesis, CIESAS, 2018.

11 Castañeda, *In the Museum*, pp. 97-130.

12 For standarization effect, see Star and Griesemer, op. cit.; for abstraction see Miller op. cit.; for time allocation (chronotopy, allochronism) see Fabian op. cit.

13 Secká, Milena, "Vojta Nápsrtek, Vlastenec, Sběratel, Mecenáš", Národní Muzeum, 2011; Scická, Milena, "Vojta Náprstek, his Museum and Library", *Annals of the Náprstek Museum in Prague*, 19, 1998: 83-88.

14 Klápšt'ová, Kateřina, "Czech Americans and their American Indian Collections from the Late Nineteenth Century at the Náprstek Museum, Part I", Annals of the Náprstek Museum in Prague 28, 2007: 171-176; Klápšt'ová, Kateřina, "North and Middle America", Annals of the Náprstek Museum in Prague 21, 2000: 1-21; Klápšt'ová, Kateřina, "The Mexican Collections at the Náprstek Museum as Witnesses of History", *Annals of the Náprstek Museum in Prague 32*,

2011: 3-14; Národní Muzeum -Náprstkovo Muzeum, Mexické Umění z Českých Sbírek, 1999.

15 See Secká, Milena, "Vojta Náprstek, Vlastenec"; Secká, Milena "Vojta Náprstek", and Národní Muzeum, The Náprstek Museum of Asian, African and American Cultures, A Guidebook, 2000.

16 See, Bohüm, Bohumil & Bohüm, Vladimír, "Preliminary Report on the Analisys on the Prague Codex deposited in the Collections of the Náprstek Museum in Prague", *Annals of the Náprstek Museum in Prague* 24, 2003: 1-12.

17 Anderson, Benedict, op. cit.

18 See, for example, Azuela, Alicia, *Arte y Poder*, México, El Colegio de Michoacán, 2013; López, Haydé, *En busca del alma nacional*, México, Instituto Nacional de Antropología e Historia, 2018; López, Paula, *Los indígenas de la nación*, México, Fondo de Cultura Económica, 2017; Pérez Montfort, Ricardo, "Un nacionalismo sin nación aparente (La fabricación de lo "típico" mexicano 1920-1950)", Política y Cultura, núm. 12, 1999, pp. 177-193.

19 Sukikara, Fumiko, *Formación y transformación en la narrativa del Popol Vuh: las publicaciones y las prácticas de traducción al japonés, 1928-1971*, Master Thesis, Universidad Autónoma de Chiapas, 2019.

20 Miller, David, op. cit.

21 Grosz, Elizabeth, op. cit.

22 Laermans, Rudy, and Pascal Gielen, "The archive of the digital an-archive", *Image & Narrative*, 17, 2007.
http://www.imageandnarrative.be/inarchive/digital_archive/laermans_gielen.htm.

23 Durkheim, Émile, "The dualism of human nature and its social conditions", in *On Morality and Society: Selected Writings*, edited by Robert N. Bellah, Chicago: Chicago University Press, 1973 [1914], pp. 149-166, p. 159.

24 De Martino, Ernesto, "Crisis of presence and religious reintegration", *Hau: Journal of Ethnographic Theory*, 2 (2), 2012 [1956], pp. 434-450, p. 443.

25 Ibid.

26 De Martino, Ernesto, *La fine del mondo: Contributo all'analisi delle apocalissi culturali* [The end of the world: Contribution to the analysis of cultural apocalypses], Edited by Clara Gallini, Torino: Einaudi, 1977, p. 136 (my translation). See also: Cometa, Michele, "*Non finito*: The form of Italian cultural studies", in *New Perspectives in Italian Cultural Studies. Volume I: Definitions, Theory, and Accented Practices*, edited by Graziella Parati, Madison:Fairleigh Dickinson University Press, 2012, pp. 19-52. On the reception of Ernesto de Martino in Japan see Uemura, Tadao, "Ernesto De Martino in Japan", *Nostos*, 1, 2016, pp. 113-128.

http://rivista.ernestodemartino.it/index.php/nostos/article/view/13.

27 "(...) to say "history" means, in the first place, to say "society," that is – at least for human societies – a mode of collective organization for the technical domination of nature; in order for society to be disclosed to law and ethics, poetry and science. (...) If the technical sphere is poor and elementary, if nature dwarfs it with its excessive power; and if retrospection is narrow and prospective consciousness of effective behaviors for the dominion over natural forces is limited; if in the interior of human society particular groups stand like "nature" in relation to certain others – that is lowered to a function which is merely technical and instrumental – then, for these very reasons, the limitation and fragility of presence as the free power to surmount situations arises, and the risk of radical alienation becomes huge. In this diffuse atmosphere of existential precariousness the process of becoming is punctuated by moments of crisis in which historicity "protrudes" and presence risks not being-there" (De Martino, Ernesto, "Crisis of presence and religious reintegration", op. cit., p. 442).

28 See Miller, David, op. cit., who also refers to immateriality of money and finances.

29 See, for example, Appadurai, Arjun, *Fear of Small Numbers*, Duke University Press, 2006.

30 See, for example, Gupta, Ahkil and James Ferguson, "Beyond "Culture": Space, Identity, and the Politics of Difference", *Cultural Anthropology*, Vol. 7, No. 1, *Space, Identity, and the Politics of Difference* (Feb. 1992), pp. 6-23.

31 For a similar view, based on Jonna Bornemark's review of De Cusa's notions of Ratio & Intellectus, of see Larsson, Martin, "Hacia una nueva historiografía. De la historia del presente a la filosofía con gente adentro", LiminaR. Estudios Sociales y Humanísticos, vol. XVIII, núm. 1, enero-junio de 2020, pp. 36-48.

32 Boltanski Luc, and Eve Chiapello, *The New Spirit of Capitalism*, London-New York: Verso, 2005 [1999].

33 https://www.archiviomemoriemigranti.net/

34 Chambers, Iain, De Angelis, Alessandra, Ianniciello, Celeste, Orabona, Mariangela and Michaela Quadraro (eds.), *The Postcolonial Museum: The Arts of Memory and the Pressures of History*, Farnham: Ashgate, 2014.

35 Kidron, Carol, "Toward an Ethnography of Silence. The Lived Presence of the Past in the Everyday Life of Holocaust Trauma Survivors and Their Descendants in Israel", *Current Anthropology*, 50 (1), 2009, pp. 5-27.

36 Ibid. p. 11.

Part 1 【概要】

記録のメディア性

　第1部「記録（archive）のメディア性」は、「モノ」が特定の価値を帯びて「記録」となり、その蓄積、伝播、リメイク／コピーを通じて現代世界の認識を形成していく様相について議論した。古い事物は考古学を筆頭とする科学的調査の対象としてのみならず、観光の目玉にもなるし、ナショナリスティックなレトリックや心象風景の根拠とされることもある。「モノ」がそのような特定の意味を付与されるまでに、壮大なリメイクの過程を経なければならないことは見過ごされがちだ。紙、石、岩、風景、工芸品、そして人間も含めた生物やその遺骸に不均衡に作用する価値と物質性の枠組み（frame）が存在しているのである。ホセ・ルイス・エスカロナ・ヴィクトリアが「政治的認識論と現代世界の形成（Political Epistemology and the Making of the Contemporary World）」と題する報告のなかで、このような枠組みの諸相と、それが現代世界にどのような帰結をもたらしてきたか、特に現在の政治的認識論への影響について研究報告を行い、コメンテーターのジャンルカ・ガッタが応答し、その後フロアとの熱気ある意見交換や議論が展開された。

　モノは物質としてあるのみならず、光、音、動き（時間）を伴いながらときには商品として交換価値を備え、またときには手放せないアイテムとして、感情を喚起する。モノの意味はアレンジされ、統制され、分配され、披露される特定のあり方—フレイミング—によって可能となる。特にわかりやすいのは博物館、考古学の現場、歴史景観都市などで、特別な建造物や場所とモノの関係が経験を作り、刺激を生み出す効果がある。自然史博物館などは、まるで時空を旅することのできる巨大なタイムマシーンのようだ。ホンジュラスのコパン・ルイナスにあるデジタル博物館では、古代遺跡の廃墟をデジタルで修復し、消えたヒエログリフを再現するなど、過去が現在に織り込まれた体験をすることができる。その体験が「現実の生活」である場合もある。チアパス高地のシナカンタンに行けば、先住民の家庭で生活体験ができるし、実際に使用されてい

50

る道具で日常性を味わえるが、それらは全て予め用意された（staged）アイテムを使っているにすぎず、その「文化的空間」は本質においてディズニーランドと大差はない。

科学的対象

　モノに関する科学的視座は、何も専門の研究者だけが持つわけではない。新しい知識、紙、音声映像資料、実験のためのサンプル、データベース、イメージ、それら全ては一度図書館、資料庫、博物館に収蔵され、利用可能な形態にリメイクされ、今度は専門家以外にも多様な形態でアクセス可能なモノとなる。特に教育と学習の過程によって科学的知識は系統立てられ、価値を付与され、専門分野の知識の厚みを増す一方で、科学的実践による知識伝達が正当化される。乱雑で断片的なカオスが抽象化された概念、図面、公式、公準へと枠付けられるが、このフレイミングは一貫した線上性や論理ではなく、むしろ誤解、論争、不安定化を内包しているのである。

断絶

　チェコ共和国のプラハに19世紀に建てられたナープルステク博物館は、アジア、アフリカ、アメリカの文物を収蔵し、紹介する博物館である。ボヘミアに生まれたチェコ・ナショナリストのヴォイタ・ナープルステクによって作られたこの博物館は、19世紀のナショナリズムの時代、ハプスブルグ帝国崩壊の時代、ナチス統治時代、共産主義時代とそれ以降で、同じ文物と同じ記録が異なる方向でフレイミングされた例である。一方では文明、産業化、技術を称揚するために機械装置や道具を集め、近代性を展示してきた空間が、他方でアフリカ、アジア、ネイティヴ・アメリカンの民俗性を表す文物を展示する民族学的性格が強いものになってきた。技術と文明の博物館から、非ヨーロッパの文化を紹介する博物館へと変わったのである。

真正性と信頼性

　ここで生じる問題は、モノの真正性である。19世紀の土産物が古代マヤ写本として展示された例があったが、それが古代メキシコ文化の有力な証拠とし

て展示されると、マヤを一部に取り入れたメキシコという国民国家の正当性につながることがある。

　建国神話や民族神話だけではなく、近代国家の物語もまた、博物館、考古学の発掘現場、歴史的景観や公文書記録を証拠品として流用することがある。革命後のメキシコの壁画や絵画、音楽は、抽象化された全体としての国家や民族がアートを通じて一般知識となっていったことを示している。メキシコ的なもの／メキシコ人であること（Mexicanhood）を作り上げるために、壁画運動は重要な役割を果たしている。しばしばピラミッドなどのマヤ遺跡や文物から取られた壁画のモティーフは、美学的、知性的であると同時に極めて政治的なものだ。メキシコ的な美学は、戦後の一時期の日本のアート・シーンにも輸入された。

　モノに関わる科学的知識は政治的美学的装置へと転生する。確かに古代マヤにおける生贄の事実はその儀礼的現場の発掘等で明らかになってはいるが、メル・ギブソンの映画「アポカリプト」（2006年公開）において描かれたマヤにおける階層性の問題は、現地で調査をすすめる人類学者たちを当惑させることになった。生贄となる者たちと生贄の儀式を司るエリート階層のあいだに決定的な分断があったような描写があるからである。フィクショナルかノンフィクショナルかを問わず、リメイクの過程には真正性と同時に信頼性の問題が常に付きまとう。

フレイミングと政治的認識論

　モノはそれ自体では決して完結せず、常に余地を残す。フレイミングは、その余地の作り方でもある。解釈と理解の道案内をするのである。博物館、テーマパーク、考古学の発掘現場、記録文書はすべて、モノを一定の枠組みによって選別し、それによってモノを経験することの一部だ。現実と物質性の経験としての認識論は、このようなモノの枠付の仕方を研究することにより明らかにされるだろう。

　知、権力、物質性に関するこのエスカロナの報告に対し、討論者のガッタはまずフレイミングを取り上げ、モノの意味を固定し、組織化し、安定させる枠組み自体の生成のされ方に疑問を呈した。フレイミングはカオスやパニックを

消去することでもあるが、それが同時にモノを脱神話化しモノの物質性を顕にする過程ならば、その分析自体がモノとどのような関係を取り結ぶのか？　フレイムの分析はどのような意味の安定化をもたらすのか？　国民化や民族化からカオスを取り戻すことはできるのか？　新たな政治的認識論を作り上げることができるのか？　ここで分析された秩序の構築過程と、物質性のカオスと秩序の間にはどのような関係があるのか？

　ガッタはさらに問う。フレイミングの政治性の事例としてあげられたナープルステク博物館において、ヨーロッパ文明と技術を展示することと、非ヨーロッパ地域の文物を展示することの根本的な違いは何か、果たしてそれは対立する方向性なのだろうか？　図書館と公文書記録とは同じ地平には立たず、それぞれに知の階層性があるのではないか？　近年の記録のデジタル化は知の階層性をなくしてはいないが、弱めてはいるように思われる。こうした技術的革新が知の階層性に及ぼす影響は、調査者と調査対象となる記録の関係性も変容させているだろう。

　ガッタが提示するもう一つの重要な問題は、フレイミング自体に秘匿性が宿るということである。博物館に展示されてしまうと、モノは日常性から切り離されて鑑賞と調査の対象となる。そのとき、イタリアの人類学者エルネスト・デ・マルティーノが言う秘匿性の技術的機能について考えねばならない。展示されることは歴史から剥離されて、モノ自体は時空間を旅することを禁じられる一方で、鑑賞者や調査者は、むしろその展示によって時空間を横断する旅をすることができる。これはある種の神話的儀礼性の具現化であり、儀礼には明かされてはいけないからくり、秘匿性が必須なのである。

　ガッタの論争的な質問群（ガッタの言う「カオス」）に対し、エスカロナは固定化された世界認識の構築方法＝フレイムを変える二つの方法に言及した。一つはマルクス主義的な革新的で変革の目的を内在化させた社会科学の方法、もう一つは現象学的なアナキズムによって世界を壊す＝カオスを作り出す方法である。また、ナープルステク博物館の方向性について、ガッタの指摘を受けたエスカロナは、文明の称揚と多文化の称揚とが対立するのではなく、展示される知としての階層性の問題だという認識に改める場面も見られた。モノとフレイミングに関する再帰性の議論が、討論者同士の見解を再帰的に検証する機

会へと展開されたのは大きな収穫であった。

　参加者との議論は大きく三つの点をめぐって展開された。第一に記録の人為性である。記録すること自体がアイデアを物質化し、人為的に集約して情報としてアクセス可能にすることだが、それがグローバルな規模でどのように変容しているのかを観光や産業という点からどのように考えられるかという問題である。文化を保護しなければいけないというとき、厳密な選択によって保護されるべきものとそうでないものとが振り分けられる宿命にある。伝統や慣習、守らなければならないモノに対する「情動の限界」が設定される。限界を定めることがどこまで文化の民主的で平等な経験を担保することができるのかは難しいが重要な問題だ。それは非言語的なコミュニケーションというより、新しいメタ言語——例えばアート——の創出によって新しい地平を切り開くことができるのではないか。

　第二にモノの具体性が民俗や文化の証明、証拠品になるということと、そうなることによって現実の日常生活における矛盾、差別、闘争の軌跡が「文化化」されてしまう問題について話し合われた。博物館に展示されるモノや文字によって紹介される習俗が、保護されるべき、守られるべきものとして意味を与えられる一方で、アイヌやマヤという名付け自体がカオスを消去し、すでにそのようなものとして認識されている文物やそれらのイメージを喚起して、フレイム自体を強化してしまう危険性について議論が起こった。モノのみならず、そのモノに関わる人間や生活を説明し理解するためのその言葉自体がもう倉庫である。言葉自体が過去に形成されてきた言葉に積み重なってきた意味の倉庫であると同時に、それを吐き出していく装置でもあるという問題である。

　第三に、博物館や公共空間におけるモノの秩序を、もう一度カオスへと引き戻す必要があるのではないか。カオスを作り出すことによってのみ、モノの秩序を知り理解することができるのではないか。このような根源的な論点へと議論は発展していった。これはエスカロナが言う「現象学的アナキズム」の視点である。これは世界認識とはいかに人工的に作られるのか、その原点を知るために必要な手続きなのだ。エスカロナはそこにマルクスの「そこにあって当たり前だと思われているものは全て溶解する（all that is solid melts into air）」という比喩を対置し、私たちがいかに強固なフレイムによって世界認識を作り

上げてきてしまったかをまずは検証すべきであると述べた。ガッタはその議論を引き継ぎ、記録の民主化をどのように成し遂げられるのかと問う。ガッタ自身が設立に関わったローマの「移民アーカイヴ」の事例が取り上げられ、記録されようとしている側（移民／難民）がヴィデオカメラを回し、編集に携わりながら主体的に記録の作業に関わることで、記録を組織化する段階で「する」側と「される」側の不均衡差をできるだけ解消しようという試みが紹介された。またアウシュヴィッツで使われていた一つのスプーンが、どれだけ強烈な記憶の伝達を可能にしているかという事例も紹介された。それは、時間的な重なりを共有し得ない子どもたちに、ある母親がアウシュヴィッツで子供に食べ物を与えていたスプーンを手にさせることによって、特定のアイデンティティに特化されずに出来事を継承していく可能性を示している。

　抽象と具体、哲学的語彙と日常の物質性、アカデミックな振る舞いと集められ、展示され、フレイム化されたものをパブリックとして経験すること。パート1は、これらの一見対立するようにみえるカテゴリーを横断し、交差し、モノとの関係の切り結び方が世界認識を創ること、またその世界認識はカオスに戻ることによって変容可能性があることを、様々な事象や具体例を参照しながら検討する、熱の籠もった議論の場となった。（小笠原博毅）

Part 2

—

Materialism of Migrating / Crosscultural Memory

Part 2

Materialism of Migrating / Crosscultural Memory

Masato Karashima: My name is Masato Karashima. So let me introduce you the speaker Gracia Imberton Deneke from Chiapas, Autonomous University of Chiapas. Welcome to Kobe, again. Gracia-san, she has her PhD from UNAM; last year I visited there. Her previous work deals with suicide, right? in the indigenous society in Mexico. And at the moment, she is doing the tourism. Today's presentation is a part of her recent project on tourism in Chiapas. So, please do.

Gracia Imberton Deneke
Textiles, Memory and Commodification of Culture
Imberton Deneke: Good Afternoon. I would like to thank the Promis, for organizing this conference here, and also the Organization for Advanced and Integrated Research. But most of all I would like to thank Dr. Hiroki Ogasawara because he is a president of this conference and he made it possible, Thank you Hiroki. And of course Fumiko Sukikara, because she has been the link between our university and Kobe University, so thank you too.

Introduction
In this presentation I will be reflecting on indigenous textile production of rural localities in the surroundings of San Cristóbal de Las Casas, Chiapas. These textiles take us back in time to past centuries, that is, to the "traditional" clothing of men, women and children from these villages and hamlets, but they also show us a very vigorous and powerful present –and surely future-life– because the conditions of production, circulation and consumption of these garments have been modified and their use has been extended to other spaces. Textiles bear the

memory of relevant historical and relational processes in the region, which helps explain their transformation over time and how they have acquired many uses and meanings in different historical moments and social spaces.

Changes in the production, consumption and meanings of indigenous craftsmanship – hand woven and embroidered garments, in particular – in San Cristóbal have occurred in the context of global and local social transformations, mainly in relation to the collapse of subsistence agriculture, massive rural–urban migration, the development of tourism and the commodification of culture. Drawing from Karl Marx's discussion on commodities, I take up López and Marín's definition of commodification of culture as the "process by which the use-value of certain goods transforms into exchange–value, through their incorporation into the market circuit"[1]. I will trace this process historically and give an account of some of the present circumstances of textiles.

I would like to comment that my research topic is tourism and social space changes: the impact of tourism in the city. But in order to come close to the subject of this conference, which is "Materality of Archive", I decided to make textiles the central object of my presentation.

Historical Account

I would like to start with a brief account of San Cristóbal's colonial history and its relationship with the rural surroundings[2]. The town we now call San Cristóbal was founded in 1528 by a group of Spanish conquerors[3], who defeated the local groups that confronted them. From this moment on, the colonial categories to designate the inhabitants of the region emerged: the different local groups were named "Indians", and the newly arrived conquerors "Spaniards". There were also black slaves in early colonial times but this category was not as sharp as the other two, and didn't last too long. The first two categories are currently used now but have been modified: Indians became "indigenous people" and, Spaniards turned into "ladinos" or "mestizos". "Ladino" has a more cultural connotation, while "mestizo" has a biological connotation –like half-breds–, in this text I will be using "Ladinos" which is the term commonly used nowadays in San Cristobal.

In colonial San Cristóbal, Spaniards, Blacks and Indians lived together within a strict hierarchy that placed Indians at the bottom. But most of the Tzeltal and Tzotzil indigenous people were forced to live in rural hamlets close to town. San Cristobal's lands were not suitable for agriculture so the town has depended on peasant labor for produce since then[4]. Indigenous areas became a reserve of cheap and unskilled labor for the city, destined to live in poverty[5]. Several researchers have described San Cristóbal as "a parasitic city"[6] because it did not develop its own productive activities, and has always lived by dispossessing indigenous localities.

The relations between Spaniards and peasant Indians were framed in the colonial process dynamics (control and overexploitation of Indian labor, excessive collection of taxes, imposition of new forms of political and religious government, population resettlements, among others). Discrimination, subjugation, racism and contempt were the prevailing attitudes towards them.

As part of the colonial process, I want to say this because I think it is important for my subject, it is commonly stated that a particular way of dressing was imposed on each village or hamlet, so that Spaniards could exercise surveillance and control over Indians, and at the same time, distinguish themselves from them. Relying on local techniques and knowledge, Indians made and wore these costumes that later became the "traditional" dress of each village.

In this presentation I will be referring to woven garments used in the Highland hamlets in the 1960s and 1970s, all made by indigenous women. Wool skirts and wool and cotton huipiles (blouses) were the dress for women, and for men, wool chuj (jackets) and cotton shirts (Figures 1 and 2).

Changes in the 20th Century

In order to understand the commodification of indigenous handmade crafts, it is necessary to start from the second half of the 20th century. I will briefly refer to several of the socio-economic conditions and agents who had a relevant participation in this process: 1) The agricultural crisis and the emergent commodification of artisan clothing, 2) The promotion of crafts (by official institutions and anthropologists), 3) Massive migration of peasants to the city, and 4) The tourism boom.

1) Agricultural Crisis and the Emergent Commodification of Artisan Clothing

The twentieth century in the Highlands of Chiapas was marked by a strong lag in several aspects. Although San Cristóbal was the region's administrative center, the first paved road (the Panamerican Highway) connecting it to the capital city was built in 1946[7]. The local elite's main economic activity was the monopoly they ruthlessly exercised over the indigenous labor force; they created coercive mechanisms to recruit these peasants, organize and sent them to work in the haciendas and coffee plantations in the Lowlands[8]. During the first half of that century they made juicy profits from this intermediation.

In the 1950s indigenous peasant localities made a living out of subsistence agriculture (corn and beans) on small plots of land; male wage-earning jobs in coffee plantations (later on in construction); and raising farm animals (for food or occasional sale) and sheep (to obtain wool for their clothing). They also engaged in commerce on a small-scale basis, trading and selling food products, pottery, woven garments and wool to other indigenous customers in local marketplaces. In San Cristóbal they sold agricultural products, firewood, charcoal, salt[9], and bought manufactured goods (agricultural tools, fireworks, thread, needles, and liquor, etcetera). Many weavers had to rely on the market to buy wool to make their family's clothes because the sheep they owned didn't provide enough.

But in the mid-seventies and eighties the peasants' economic situation turned desperate due to a national agrarian crisis[10]. Agriculture was no longer an option and alternative jobs were scarce (wage-labor in agriculture or construction). Simultaneously there was a large population growth that complicated the situation. At this time, textile production became a new income source for some indigenous family groups.

The case of the indigenous village of Navenchauc is a good example of how handcrafted clothes were commodified[11]. In the fifties, it was common for most women in indigenous villages to weave clothes for their own family, as well as to tend a flock of sheep from which to obtain wool. They used the backstrap loom (as in pre-Hispanic times) and processed the wool manually. Occasionally they could sell a garment in San Cristóbal (to other indigenous people or to ladino stores) or even in their village, although production for family use prevailed.

But during the seventies and eighties, several ladino stores in the city became interested in buying indigenous garments (blouses –huipiles– and robes) to sell to tourists and anthropologists. Women weavers were contacted by storeowners and began to work by "assignments"[12], both for local ladino and foreigners businesses. Sometimes the merchant's "assignments" demanded a large production in a very short time so a few weavers began to organize other women to work for them, and then they became their "representatives". In other cases specialization arose because some women had more experience embroidering, for example, so they were in charge of that part of the process only.

The weavers produced "traditional" garments, but had to adapt their production to new consumers: synthetic materials were used, different items were created to the liking of tourists (tablecloths, cushion covers, table runners, napkins) and templates (stencils) for embroidery and weaving were introduced. These novelties were not available to all craftswomen, so some were forced to depend on those who had access to them. At this time, the first textiles stores in the village opened up, owned by some of the "representatives".

As a result of this, internal socioeconomic differentiation emerged in Navenchauc between those indigenous families who owned shops, organized the work of other women, and were close to the ladino and foreigner merchants, on one side, and the rest of the peasant families who did not have the means to invest in textile production, on the other. A group of families in Navenchauc then engaged mainly in the production of exchange values for the market.

2) The Promotion of Handicrafts

In the seventies, other agents played very important roles in the commodification of textile garments in the region. One of them was the National Indigenist Institute (NII), an official institution created by the Mexican state to promote the integration of "backward" and "primitive" indigenous people in the national mestizo society[13]. This policy took the name of indigenism, and sought to modernize the ethnic groups through educational programs, economic development, healthcare, among others. At the same time, the preservation of certain "positive" aspects of their cultures (handcraft production, being the most important, and festivals and rituals) was encouraged.

During this decade, the Mexican state strongly promoted handcraft production (textiles, ceramics, etc.) at a national level for two reasons. One of the goals was to stop peasants massive migration to the cities, and this required creating employment in their hamlets. But they also sought to adapt crafts production for tourist's taste. For this purpose a national program for handcrafts production and commercialization was drawn up: stores opened in 1974 (FONART), courses and workshops to improve techniques were delivered, cooperatives were promoted, contests and fairs were invented, museums opened (handicraft houses) to exhibit products. Some standards on "authenticity", "originality" and "quality" concerning traditional indigenous creations were defined and the importance of indigenous peoples as living representatives of ancient Mexicans, bearers of tradition, was highlighted. In San Cristóbal, INI organized the first local handicraft competition in 1972; FONART opened an office to buy handcrafts in 1974[14]. In 1977 the Sna Jolobil cooperative was founded, the oldest cooperative with the best quality products, by American anthropologist Walter Morris and an indigenous weaver, Pedro Meza.

Other agents that had a very strong impact on textile commercialization were a group of scholars (anthropologists and psychologists from Harvard and other universities, as well as from the NII) who carried out research on textile production in the Highlands. Several of them were part of the Harvard project headed by anthropologist Evon Vogt, who came at the invitation of the National Indigenist Institute. According to Jan Rus[15], through the Harvard Project numerous researchers and graduate students moved to Chiapas, and carried out thesis work and research mainly on indigenous groups. In general terms, they conceived indigenous people as conservative communities that sought their own isolation in order to avoid internal changes. They emphasized the "continuity" of a particular Mayan worldview, with social and cultural structures that descended directly from the pre-Hispanic period to the present day.

These scholars researched many subjects related to handcraft production, but most important for the matter at hand were their symbolic interpretations of textile designs, in search of what they conceived as the lost Mayan worldview. Anthropologist Marta Turok[16], for example, resorted to the analysis of rituals and myths (and not to ethnography), to explain symbolism in woven garments. She claimed the symbolism was not a "conscious" system for weavers, because the artisans she worked with did not ascribe these profound meanings to their designs. The narrative on textile crafts by these anthropologists stated that this particular handcraft reproduces indigenous culture, its identity, and expresses the continuity of something very profound (which anthropologists have to reveal because indigenous people are not aware of it).

Just as the Mexican state built a nationalist narrative on "authentic" tradition, anthropologists collaborated in the creation of another narrative that enhanced the forgotten and lost value of textiles, indigenous culture and identity. This narrative added new value to the textiles, in addition to the technical expertise, because it ascribed them to a millenary culture that possessed profound cosmogonic knowledge.

3) Massive Migration to San Cristóbal

Not all indigenous peasant families from the Highlands were able to insert themselves in the production and commercialization of textiles, some of them had to migrate to make a living. Initially a few came to San Cristóbal, but starting from

1976 on there was a massive migration to this city as a result of political-religious conflicts in Chamula indigenous town. In addition to the agricultural crisis and population growth that I mentioned earlier, many conflicts over land arose between indigenous and non-indigenous people, as well as harsh confrontations between indigenous people over scarce resources in their hamlets (sand banks, water sources, etc.). Important indigenous leaderships emerged that led to the violent expulsion of thousands of people, and many arrived in San Cristóbal[17].

The Sancristobalenses felt the massive arrival of "Indians" as an invasion, because they had tried to preserve their city for ladinos only. The refugees settled on the outskirts and, unable to return to their homelands, organized themselves to struggle to find jobs in the city. At the beginning of the eighties, three or four expelled women artisans asked the representatives of the Church of Santo Domingo for permission to sell their woven and embroidered garments in the park outside the church. What started as a small street market now houses more than 800 to 1,000 craft stalls. So far Santo Domingo is the only public textile market run by indigenous people.

4) Tourist Boom

Another factor that contributed to the commodification of handmade textiles was the arrival of tourism to the region. During the seventies the Mexican state boosted tourism throughout the country, responding to international organizations policies (United Nations, World Bank, Inter-American Development Bank, among others) which sought to promote "development" in Third World countries. New government offices grew in all states and resources began to flow.

San Cristobal was very appealing due to its colonial monuments and buildings, considered an expression of cultural heritage; the presence of the indigenous peoples and their handcrafts; and it's location as a passageway to archaeological and natural sites. At the end of the seventies and during the eighties, tourism began to arrive in greater numbers. But it was the Zapatista uprising of 1994 that gave tourism a significant upturn[18]. This rebellion exposed at an international and national level the harsh conditions of poverty and exploitation of Chiapas indigenous peoples. It attracted analysts, journalists, activists and tourists, many of them sympathizers or interested mainly in the indigenous people. The new social situation drew many different people to the city.

From 1994 onwards, there has been a sustained growth in the commodification of textile production: new organizations of weavers (driven by NGOs) and private indigenous enterprises dedicated to textile production emerged, and the number of established craft shops (mostly in the hands of ladinos or foreigners) increased. A decade later the first designer stores opened up.

From the seventies until 2019, tourism has been the most important bet of local governments and businessmen, who permanently resort to images, symbols and representations of indigenous people and their handcrafts in hotels, restaurants, shops, bars, etc.

Textiles Today

What are the uses and meanings of textiles today? How are the processes of circulation and consumption of these commodified textiles?

A quick visit (only through photographs) to 3 spots in the ex-convent of Santo Domingo and a fashion store in San Cristobal can help us address these questions. Santo Domingo is a space of approximately 10,000 sq. mts. that includes several heritage monuments (church, chapel, Dominican ex-convent), church and museum offices, a kiosk and a park. The ex-convent houses two museums: one is dedicated to regional history and the other to textiles: Textiles Center of the Mayan World. The former park now shelters the indigenous marketplace that includes 800 to 1,000 stalls.

1) The first is the indigenous marketplace that has grown since the eighties, overflowing what once was a public park. Indigenous people, artisans and merchants, generally wearing their "traditional" custom, sell items they have made themselves or bought from others local weavers (of not so good quality), as

well as crafts from Guatemala, other parts of Mexico, and even India. This is how they make a living. But the marketplace is considered illegal because they are using a public park for private profit, so they live under permanent threat of being evicted. Tourists like this place because of the low prices and to experience "the anthropological other" encounter (Figure 3).

2) A few meters from the marketplace, but inside the ex-convent, we find the indigenous cooperative San Jolobil, which was founded in the 1970s by an American anthropologist and a male indigenous weaver. Around 800 indigenous artisans are members of Sna Jolobil; they sell traditional clothing, but also have a novelty line for interior decoration (cushions, tablecloths, napkins), all very good quality with high prices. The items sold there include a card that registers data of its elaboration, and its work is notoriously different from that of the outsiders. The sale is aimed at consumers with greater resources. They are at no risk of being evicted (Figure 3).

3) Inside the ex-convent is the Textiles Center of the Mayan World, a museum that exhibits two private collections gathered by anthropologists, with more than 2500 garments from Chiapas and Guatemala, in modern cabinets with drawers for visitors to admire. These textiles were chosen for their quality and because they are representative of the diverse towns of Chiapas and Guatemala's Highlands. Some were made by Sna Jolobil's artisans. The visit to the museum has a cost of 3 dlls. approximately. These textiles were commodities at one time, but were left out of the circulation circuit for its beauty and finesse to become objects of exhibition (Figure 4).

Downtown streets we find:
4) Fashion stores are located in the commercial plazas or pedestrian walkways destined for tourists and the middle and high class sectors of San Cristóbal. These shops are spaces with a very careful decoration and exhibition arrangement, with

pricey garments that have incorporated indigenous textiles combined with other materials and techniques to create novel models, following international fashion trends (Figure 5).

Coming to a conclusion....Textiles in this region entered the market as exchange-values due to the economic needs of peasant families in specific circumstances: the recurrent agricultural crises, the massive and forced migrations to the city, as well as the take-off of tourism. Before there had been an occasional and sporadic mercantile exchange, but later commodification took place.

But once on the market, additional values were ascribed to textiles: official institutions highlighted the traditional indigenous character as part of national cultural heritage. Anthropologists and other scholars added a "symbolic" value to textile garments, connecting them to the indigenous world of their producers (their worldview, ways of life and identity). Museums and exhibitions were created to preserve and showcase these items, not always accounting for their production processes. Now these textiles –exchange-values– follow very different paths (we have just followed 4 paths), depending on exchange and consumption processes at local and global levels. In my opinion, these textiles carry the memory of all the processes described above. Thank you.

Karashima: Thank you very much. The anthropologists come and the textiles go, rural breachers go, refugees come and also tourists come. The museums go. Gracia shows chronologically the very dynamic interaction between knowledge, capital, tourism and also global organisations such as kind of UNESCO world heritage or something, NGO or something like that. So before going to Nakatani san's comments, I would pick up some questions on basic information, geographical information or something like that.

Public 1: Basic one. Quick question for clarification: which animal is it, I mean, garments.

Imberton Deneke: The traditional clothes I'm talking about include four basic pieces which are: huipiles, wool and cotton blouses for women; a wool cape used in Zinacantán; and the women's skirt made also of wool. These three are female garments. The fourth one is the *chuj*, which is a man's wool jacket with a belt on the waist.

Public 2: Today they use chemical fabric as well?

Imberton Deneke: Is it the industrial fabrics you mean? Yes, they use for blouses. They used to buy cotton, for now satin and other central products only for the blouses and for the skirts, not wool but one with cotton, yes, they use now even the shiny colours, with gold and silver.

Ayami Nakatani: May I start my comments now? People are already asking my questions!

Karashima: Ok, please.

Ayami Nakatani
Contextualisation of "Traditions"

Nakatani: Thank you. Someone just asked what I wanted to ask, so. Thank you, Gracia, for your intriguing paper, which is relevant to my own research concerns in many ways.

I am Ayami Nakatani from Okayama University. I'm an anthropologist, specializing in women's work and the changing process of production and consumption of traditional textiles in Asia and beyond. The outcome of my collaborative research with both Japanese and overseas scholars will be published soon. Let me share with you a few lines from the Introduction of the book:

"[T]extiles, which form an indispensable part of sartorial practice, play a decisive role in [the historical] process, as markers of status, gender, ethnicity, and religion….such boundaries are continuously negotiated, shifting, and re-created."[19]

Through critical examinations of ongoing developments, we have tried to capture the complex reality faced by producers and consumers of handmade textiles. By so doing, our case studies from different parts of Asia, including mine on Indonesia, demonstrate the multi-layered influence of often contradictory forces upon local systems of production: with traditionalist discourse emphasizing continuity of age-old practices and cultural authenticity on the one hand, and fashion and other market trends demanding constant change to ensure marketability on the other. I believe our approach and main argument have resonance with what Gracia has just described for the case of Chiapas.

Gracia's paper brilliantly explicated the multifaced nature of commodification of culture, in reference to the concrete cases of traditional textiles made and used by indigenous population in highland Chiapas. There emerged commercial production of indigenous textiles, which, as she argued, turned these textiles from the objects of use-value to those endowed with exchange value in the market. This change was necessitated by the needs of cash income among the indigenous population. Such a move was facilitated by different types of intervention, including the development efforts by the local government, the presence of anthropologists themselves as both "tourists" and "collectors" as well as researchers of indigenous culture, and of course the increasing tourism sector.

These combined factors culminated in the visualization of indigenous cultural values. In consequence, new materials, new designs and new usages have been introduced in the production of indigenous textiles. The division of labour between female producers has also emerged. At the same time, as Gracia described, we see the expansion of inequalities among indigenous population.

Now, I wonder what happened to local garments, made and worn by the residents. You have partially touched upon this issue already in response to

Hiroki's question, but I would like you to elaborate a little more on this point. What kind of sentiment do people still attach to these traditional textiles and traditional forms of outfits? Do they continue to wear conventional dress in their daily life or just put them at festivals or on some special occasions only? Do they prefer to wear Western type of clothing? How do they differentiate available styles? Do you see a different attitude among men and women? Can local population afford to buy their elaborate ethnic clothes? These are immediate questions that occurred to me.

Another point I think important and relevant to Gracia's paper is the question of authenticity. When it comes to the act of ensuring authenticity, a question arises: are we most concerned with the forms, fabrics, materials or styles of wearing? What we should wear must have evolved over time, thus any attempt of pinning down a particular style of clothing at any particular moment in history is inevitably an arbitrary act despite our inclination to call it traditional or authentic. When we try to preserve or revive certain practices as our tradition, these practices are time-bound; how far should we go back in history depends on our arbitrary decision.

Let me give you an example. Among Hmong women in Wenshan, Yunnan Province situated in southwestern part of China, it was customary for them to wear clothes that they made by themselves. The production process was lengthy and painstaking, ranging from growing hemp, spinning its extracted fibers into threads, weaving threads with a back-strap loom to make a fabric, to decorating the fabric with *batik* technique, pleating and embroidery (Figure 6). Decorated pieces were finally sewn together by hand. In the 1980s and 1990s, however, women gradually turned to factory-made fabrics, brightly colored yarns and sewing machines and eventually ready-made garments sold in the market or shops. Those newly available clothes are still deemed as a Hmong-style, special outfit for festivities during the New Year season, yet their materials, colors, and forms are radically different from conventional styles, entirely made by hands (Figure 7). Young women, in particular, are very much concerned with the latest fashion; they want to wear something different from their peers. In the eyes of outsiders, their act may be seen as something like a "cosplay." However, despite such a rapture from "tradition," these dresses endowed with "new style" continue to represent their ethnic identity vis-à-vis the majority population of China and other ethnic minority groups.[20] More recently, it is said that even the majority Han Chinese have started to buy these costumes and wear them at parties. How should we understand such a phenomenon?

In a sense, ethnic/national costumes can be easily turned into the items of "cosplay" as we see in Kyoto or Seoul, where international tourists stroll around in their rented *kimono* or *hanbok*. Even my son, who never had a chance to wear kimono previously, was genuinely excited about putting on *yukata* (summer-style *kimono*) provided by the Japanese-style inn (*ryokan*). He could be excited as much as international tourists can be in the sense that he himself was very much distanced from Japanese national costume in his daily context.

But today, there is another example I would like to talk about in my efforts of matching with the theme of Gracia's talk. It's about material representation of objects made by Ainu people of Japan.

First of all, who is "Ainu"? Ainu literally means "human being": they resided in northern Japan (Hokkaido, Sakhalin and Kurile island) prior to the arrival of the mainland Japanese. However, they were deprived of lands, resources, language and other cultural traditions, after the mainland Japanese migrated and governed on these islands. As a result of further assimilation policies, it is believed that full-blood Ainu no longer exists. Today, there is no legal definition for Ainu. A survey by the local government of Hokkaido defined Ainu as those who "are considered to have Ainu bloodline and those who reside with Ainu people due to marriage, adoption and so forth."[21] So if you inherit a drop of blood, you can be identified as Ainu. Alternatively, you may not be categorized as Ainu by bloodline, but if you have a long-standing relationship with Ainu by living with them as a foster child, for example, you can claim to be Ainu.

But even for those who inherit Ainu blood or culture traditions, there are still difficulties for them to identify themselves as Ainu publicly due to the fear of potential discrimination. In addition to the rigorous assimilation policy enforced by the colonizers, the existence of such discrimination against Ainu also contributed to the fact that Ainu cultural traditions including language, music and dance, or various forms of material culture were not properly handed down. Ainu descendants often concealed their identities from Japanese major society or even from their spouses if they married a Japanese. Therefore, even those who are fully aware of their ancestral connection with Ainu would also shy away from Ainu cultural practices, because they were afraid of being stigmatized or bullied in the neighbouring communities or in the wider society.

But the installation of a new legislation called "Ainu Cultural Protection Law" in 1997 made a turning point. This law replaced the former notorious law: "Former Aborigines (*dojin*) Protection Law." The new law met the demands from Ainu people only partially, for it did not address their indigenous rights, but at least the government subsidies became available for the promotion of Ainu traditional culture, including Ainu language lessons and the transmission of craft skills such as textile production and wood carving.[22] In 2009, Advisory Council for Future Ainu Policy issued a report; it acknowledged the deprivation of Ainu lands, resources and cultural traditions, and proposed measures to grant "access to natural resources as an element in protecting and transmitting traditional culture," yet its emphasis was limited to cultural dimensions of Ainu ways of life.[23] In this vein, it invited critical responses from Ainu activists who have fought for their rights. Below is one such remark cited by Tessa Morris-Suzuki.

"We Ainu wanted the restoration of the rights that had been taken away from us, and demanded various things. In the end this turned out just to be a law to promote culture, but all the same it has great meaning as a first step in a new law recognising the Ainu people,... [But] we Ainu thought this was a law for the Ainu people. We hoped that when this law was created it would bring great benefits to Ainu. We called for education and culture, the elimination of discrimination, employment measures, an autonomy fund and many things. But the law that has been passed is an Ainu culture law. This is not a law that Ainu alone can make use of. Rather, it benefits wajin [non-Ainu Japanese]. For example, any groups or individuals who conduct research or run cultural events on Ainu can apply for [financial] support [under the law] ..."[24]

There is another law enforced in May 24, 2019: "Act on Promoting Measures to Realize a Society in Which the Pride of the Ainu People Is Respected." This new act stipulates that the government should adopt policies to facilitate people's understanding of the Ainu traditions and the importance of diversity within our society. In addition, "the national government is to subsidize local government efforts to preserve the traditional culture of the Ainu."[25]

As a consequence of these legal measures and promotions, now we can see a variety of cultural practices richly exhibited in various museums in Hokkaido. This can be the most visible effect of these new laws, though the general public's exposure to Ainu cultures is still very limited compared with the cases of Australia or Canada.

Two types of handicrafts, wooden trays decorated with carving (*Ita*) and woven textiles (*Attus*), were designated as items of Traditional Craft Industries (*Dento teki Kogeihin*) by the Ministry of Trade, Economy and Industry under the Act on the Promotion of Traditional Craft Industries. There are several criteria for such designations such as that those craft items have been produced at least for hundred years old and have to be made by hand, etc. So far, only two items are designated as such for Hokkaido prefecture.

One of the designated items is Ainu traditional textiles called *Attus*, woven with yarn processed from inner bark of *at-ni*, lobed elm (*Ulmus laciniata*).[26] One of its defining features is a lengthy process of making yarns from natural materials. That particular aspect of Ainu culture is appealing to the Japanese, especially for *kimono* fans. For example, a Japanese women's magazine exclusively devoted to the kimono culture published a feature article on *Attus*. The article titled, "Visiting

Attus weaving in Nibutani: fabrics born from trees, nurtured by Ainu, who live with nature,"[27] describes in detail the methods of processing yarns from harvesting barks, soaking inner barks in the water, splitting inner barks and twisting them into threads, and to colour them with natural dyes and weaving fabrics with a back-tension loom. It is said that making yarns takes up 90% of the whole cloth making procedures; this makes the end-price of fabrics very high.

Although *Attus* textile is originally meant for Ainu traditional clothing, its producers now mainly weave *obi* (*sash*) to match mainland-Japanese style kimono. The obi I saw in a department store in Tokyo was sold at 5,800 US dollars per piece. The similar cases can also be observed for handwoven textiles in the islands of Okinawa, southern most region of Japan. Certain traditional skills that used to be employed for producing daily or festive clothing of local population can only be sustained today by producing luxury items for the majority population. As I noted elsewhere, marketability is one of the key issues for the conservation of intangible cultural heritage.[28]

There is another example related to this issue. *Saranip*, a hand-woven carry bag for harvesting and storing grains or other natural resources, is another popular item made from inner bark of *at-ni* trees. The Ainu women go through the same process of producing yarn, but they use a different tool to weave *saranip*. Rather recently, one of Tokyo-based fashion stores commissioned an Ainu artist to create a new style of *saranip* bags, that cater for its young customers. The artist herself has a memory of *saranip* in its original context: she remembers how her grandmother was using a traditional loom to produce them and how they were used in their daily life. She seems to have tried to bridge her own memories and understanding of Ainu culture and the market needs solicited by the select shop, which was her client. The result is tote bags, made of Nepalese organic hemp, that may appeal to the youth living an urban life.

The use of hemp, instead of *at-ni*, must be a decision out of necessity; the production cost should be kept low enough to make the bags affordable for young clients.

This particular project was well-publicized and the detailed information about Ainu material culture and original usage of *saranip* and other craft items that were featured on this occasion was disseminated via website. In this respect, a modernized and radically modified version of traditional containers/bags may serve as a window for the general public to understand some aspect of Ainu culture. At least the artist, who created these bags in the contemporary and commercial context, carries legacy and she recognizes connection with her ancestors. Nevertheless, when I compare two objects that are very much different in forms, materials, and usages, a question comes to my mind: in what ways can we ensure cultural continuity in the sense of transmission of craft skills and their products?

As Hiroki mentioned briefly, Upopoy, the National Ainu Museum and Park, will be open next year, just in time for the Tokyo Olympic Games. This institution is also called "the symbolic space for ethnic harmony." We wonder what kind of harmony are they going to stage? Naturally, the positioning of each object and the positioning of each material culture will be designed by the organisers of museum. I know the planning and organization of this museum exhibition has involved some expert of Ainu researchers, curators and artists as well. Yet given the fixed context, the objects will also give the fixed meaning; it may be difficult to understand hidden messages and hidden memories embedded in those objects.

Now let me come back to my questions to Gracia. I tell you the reasons why I wanted to ask you these questions. In my view, at the end of the day, what makes a particular, contemporary and marketable object authentic is what I call "cultural proximity." To what extent the producers of particular craft items can relate themselves to the products they create? Are there any connection or lived relationships between what they produce for the market and what they produce for themselves?

As much as I know from the literature, in some parts of Mesoamerica some producers are very successful in making indigenous textiles and products for sale. But they often do not wear them any longer; they are already modernised, they have money, so they don't have to wear these indigenous textiles. They are making them simply for sale in the world market. The same thing is happening in Asia. In some cases, however, the producers still see the meaning of the textiles; they can relate themselves to particular textiles that used serve certain ritual purposes, for example, yet they now produce them for sale. But if such connections are lost, I think these material objects will no longer carry the meaning or memories. That's my point. Thank you.

Karashima: Thanks Nakatani-san. Gracias-san, any comments?

Q&A

Imberton Deneke: Thank you for your presentation. It was very interesting and absolutely related to my own presentation. I think many things are going on at the same time. It seems to me that textile production in Chiapas has taken different paths, as I have tried to show in my presentation. To begin with, I will distinguish between production that indigenous people of Chiapas Highlands carry out for their own use from production for the market. Many indigenous people continue to use clothing referred to as "traditional," this means that production for sale has not made production for their own use disappear. Some use them on a daily basis, others only for special occasions (ceremonial). Traditional clothing is expensive and difficult to make. Also among indigenous people there is buying and selling of handcrafted pieces because not all women know how to weave or not all do it equally well, and this has been happening for decades, it is not a recent phenomenon.

What is important to note is that "traditional" clothing woven by indigenous women for indigenous people has undergone important changes as well. New materials have been incorporated (synthetics, metal threads), a different and greater use of colors, and new techniques (embroidery machine). For example, in the town of Zinacantán women have covered traditional skirts and blouses with colorful flowers and animals that they make with embroidery machines, and they are very proud of these changes. They do not think they are giving up their culture, roots or tradition, they see them as positive changes and are recognized in the village for their creativity and talent. By this I mean that production for own use is also dynamic and changing, the designs of the past are not reproduced mechanically, it is accepted that these can change. This is where the discussion about authenticity comes in. Are these new garments not indigenous? If they are not the designs of the past (which were also imposed by the Spanish), then are they no longer indigenous? Who can tell what is or isn't original?

On the other hand, we have production of textiles for tourists, which has led to the adaptation to tastes and needs of non-indigenous buyers. Traditional garments such as the huipiles have been adapted as commodities: colors and their combinations have been attenuated, the neck has been made bigger, among others. In addition, new pieces were created: table runners, cushions, napkins, women's bags, scarves. All these garments are destined to the tourist market mainly, very few indigenous people use them.

But in production for the market - in commodification - several agents have intervened, in addition to indigenous people: the Mexican State through development institutions, as well as indigenous and non-indigenous merchants (Mexican and foreign), fashion designers, publicists, academics, NGOs, among others. Indigenous women continue to produce textiles, but the conditions depend on where and how they take part of it: as wage labourers, business owners, subjects of official credits, managers within cooperatives, vendors, etcetera.

This is what I mean when I say that there are many processes going on simultaneously and that textiles keep the memory of them. By memory I am not highlighting some symbolic content assigned in the past to these garments, transmitted from generation to generation, but rather I am pointing to the history of the transition of use values into exchange values or commodities, tracing the different paths they have followed. For this reason I do not analyze this process in terms of a cultural loss or disconnection, but rather of social agents inserted in capitalist relations of production.

The process of commodification of textiles must also be analyzed considering the subordinate position of indigenous people in the broader society of the Chiapas highlands. As a result of the discrimination, abuse, and humiliation they suffered over the centuries, the Tsotsil and Tseltal who migrated to the city in the second half of the 20th century had to hide their origins and language, as well as change their clothing in order not to be mistreated. This caused the emergence of the so-called "revestidos", indigenous people dressed as ladinos, who sought to go unnoticed in San Cristobal; the abandonment of traditional clothing was a survival strategy.

But the massive migration of indigenous people in the 1970s and 1980s and the subsequent uprising of the Zapatista Army of National Liberation (EZLN) in 1994 changed the relationship between indigenous people and ladinos in the city in various ways. There are now numerous indigenous neighborhoods where many wear traditional clothing and their language is spoken publicly. And the Zapatista uprising, which aroused great interest and support nationally and internationally, resulted in greater strength and dignity of the indigenous people in the region.

Karashima: I will welcome comments and questions from all of you.

Public 3: Thank you very much. Very beautiful presentation. I think starting with objects with José Luis first, it's very interesting, and also useful to materialize social structure and social dynamics. I'm curious to know something more about the other subject you mentioned, the boundary of historical root between *Ladinos* and indigenous people, and the presence of American anthropologist and tourist later. So the presentation of the trajectory of the indigenous people is quite geared, also how the commodification of textile affected their social style, social sophistication, differentiation due to production dynamics. But, I'm wondering which is the role of *Ladinos* on the demand side. When you talk about the middle classes and upper middle classes are you talking about *Ladinos* or also indigenous successful leaders and producers?; so how the cultural consumption of this kind of textiles affects everyday life of *Ladino* people or is there tension, conflict around this product? And also who are tourists; where they come from, Mexican people or international people. And if the surprise is so differentiated, interesting of European market, the more artistic subjectified production, modern product maybe reflect the differentiation of surplus side. So I would like to ask you, especially about the role of *Ladinos*, in this kind of market.

Imberton Deneke: Until the 1950's, indigenous people could not live in the city, nor stay there at night (unless they worked in the house of some ladino or foreigner). They came to San Cristobal to work or to sell and buy only. They usually sold agricultural products in the market or on the streets and bought manufactured products (thread, needles, and some knitting instruments, among many others) in ladino stores that were geared to indigenous peasants. These stores were owned by ladino women, and relationships with Indian buyers were abusive in terms of price and treatment. Some anthropologists, such as Marta Turok, point out that merchants exchanged liquor for handicrafts (or that they got the Indians drunk and then did not pay them). Occasionally indigenous women, with some pressing need, sold these merchants some handcrafted garment made by them.

In the 1970s, when tourists and more anthropologists began to arrive, the merchants realized that visitors were interested in buying traditional woven clothing. So they started asking the craftswomen to produce these pieces. Answering the public's question, these ladinas played a fundamental role in the first moments of commodification of these garments, as I explained in the presentation, before the arrival of state institutions, and long before fashion stores, NGOs, cooperatives.

San Cristóbal has received different types of tourism. According to the work of anthropologist Pierre van den Berghe, in the early 1950's mainly resourceful American adventurers were arriving to tour Guatemala and southern Mexico. In the 1960s and 1970s, backpackers began to arrive, mostly young Europeans who travelled with few economic resources, attracted by Mayan groups, archaeological sites and nature. They made San Cristobal fashionable as an alternative hippie destination. In the 80's, all-inclusive tours began to proliferate, with large groups of tourists from all over the world (Israel, European countries, United States, Australia, New Zealand, among others). But the strongest impulse to tourism came from the Zapatista uprising of 1994: tourists in solidarity with the movement, journalists, academics, NGOs had a strong presence in the city.

Public 4: Thank you for the presentation. I have one or maybe two questions for you, because I'm more concerned on the use of indigenous, like how they are involved in this process; first question is like, how are they involved in this process like making textiles and how they sell them? And the second question is; the textile itself can, maybe, say, pass memories from parents generations to other generations, do they also (pass) through this making process, they also are aware of those passed memories and try to keep them and maybe pass down to their next generation? That's my simple questions, because your presentation is very much focused on the product itself and the commercial topics. Thank you.

Imberton Deneke: With regard to the symbolic content of the textiles and how this has been passed on from generation to generation, I can say the following. A group of anthropologists (Marta Turok and Walter Morris) did research in the seventies on the meanings of indigenous designs. The weavers they worked with had no knowledge of these symbols. They knew the names of the figures (toad, scorpion, butterfly), but they did not relate them to a Mayan cosmovision. It was the anthropologists who elaborated these symbolic connections drawing from the study of rituals, mythology and pre-Hispanic figures in archaeological sites. For example, they say that the world is conceived as a rhombus (diamond) and each corner is a cardinal direction and this is reflected in the shape of the huipiles (blouses). Turok argues that the symbolic system among contemporary indigenous people is unconscious; I am not clear then how it can be passed on from generation to generation.

Technical knowledge, on the other hand, is transmitted from mother to daughter. The backstrap loom dates from pre-Hispanic times and has been maintained to the present day. Generally, mothers make little girls (5-6 years old) watch carefully when they weave. Learning is based more on observation and imitation than on oral explanations. They then make toy looms for the girls to experience what they have observed. The mother or older sister will be watching from a distance and helping out only when necessary. Good weavers are widely recognized in their hamlets.

Public 5: I'm from Kobe University and I want to ask about the meaning of making process in this weaving garments or textiles, because when we want to sell commodity, we have to make our product listening with the consumers or the buyer's expectations. For example, the countries like ex-colonised countries specially have these tendency to be seen with this essentialist marker or essentialist manner because, for example Kyoto, sorry to mention Kyoto so much, I don't like Kyoto actually; like Kyoto they have this kind of attitude because they try to answer their expectation from foreigners like the foreigners have this image of Kyoto, like traditional and for some really progressive, I really don't understand what they mean, but that's the image of Kyoto and they make themselves as their identities and commodify themselves, Kyoto itself. So I want to know in Chiapas is there any kind of essentialism and is there any point or something that he gets when you see the weaving process or when you see the product whether to get resonance with the essentialism. I just wonder the meaning of making process.

Karashima: If you have another question, please raise your hand. Ok, actually I would like to have a coffee break at 3:30. So I will collect questions and comments together.

Public 5: I'm totally out of the order, I'm not scholar or researcher so my question maybe out of place. Thank you for the interesting presentations. Just because I don't have any background on the period, I couldn't help feeling a certain sense of anxiety or ambivalence about the word, "indigenous" on the presentations, something like that. And I'm wondering where is the start; or firstly am I rightly sensing that? When you use the word indigenous. Yes a certain kind of break. I'm on your side that why I couldn't sense. But, if there is right, then my question is where is the start of step normal; are you worried about for the producers of these indigenous goods that they are not dearly no longer indigenous and they are being gulled, or are you worried that yourself as a researcher, there is no longer indigenous materials or space to move forward with your researches, or for the consumers we accord like these indigenous or traditional things or indigenous and traditional those are ambivalent words; are you worried for the consumers, the neighbours. Or for something else. That's my question.

Imberton Deneke: Answering the (first) question, yes, the risks of essentialism are very present when talking about indigenous ethnic groups. Essentializing means attributing basic, particular, constitutive qualities to these groups, practically conceived as "natural" traits. They are presented as static societies, that show continuity throughout centuries, and act as a homogeneous unit, without differences, inequalities or conflicts, always defined in opposition to others.

The same essentialist ideas can be applied to textiles made by indigenous people. They can be thought of as an expression of the complex Mayan worldview, original and authentic, and changes will be considered as cultural loss, withdrawal, or aggression against it. But indigenous groups also take advantage of these stereotypes or preconceived ideas. For example, in Zinacantan some indigenous families promote "visits" to their homes so that tourists can have a close experience with "the other". They display a weaver using the backstrap loom, the altar inside the house, give them a taste of the local food and drink, and finally show them the clothes that are for sale. They make a performance for visitors to find what they want to see: they hide all household appliances, mobile phones, etc. to project the idea of not being contaminated by modernity. And by doing this they have more sales and profits.

Sometimes ethnic groups or organizations can resort to essentialist ideas as a political strategy, for example, to support historical claims over the territory from which they were stripped. That is a different situation. I find it is important to keep away from essentialist ideas and to analyze these groups in their particular historical and political dimension, and to think that these essentialist positions are in fact a social construction that must be dismantled.

And about the second comment, no, my intention was to show the recent history (since 1950) of hand woven textile production of indigenous people of Chiapas, and to explain how it was gradually incorporated by the capitalist market logic, being transformed into a commodity. In this process, women artisans do not have a significant weight in the decisions and direction of the process; it is the other agents involved (the state, merchants, designers, among others), those who have the economic, material and human resources, who have a preponderant role. The craftswomen can become salaried workers or sell their products on their own. In only a few cases have they been able to start successful businesses that allow them to thrive economically.

My idea was to talk about textiles as objects that show a particular history – the transition from use values to exchange values – not only of indigenous craft production, but of the relationships between indigenous people, Ladinos, state institutions, merchants and tourists, among others, in Los Altos de Chiapas.

Public 6: This case is fabrication maybe for selling. Because there is an official identity for them so they have to make it. They have double life.

Imberton Deneke: In the case of the crafts market in San Cristobal, indigenous sellers know that tourists want to see traditional cloths and people. So vendors always wear these garments when they are there. Maybe when they leave they will change and use other "western" clothes. In that sense you can say they are doing a representation of what tourists want to see.

Public 6: Because like you mentioned, there is an attraction what the tourists have to pay, so the meaning of making process itself is not all about the money, capital.

Imberton Deneke: I think it is, because in the end they sell the goods. They have other textiles or garments, things there, so if you go to their houses you have the advantage to visit their homes but that can make you feel obliged to buy something; you are not paying an entrance fee but you usually buy something. You don't have to, but it's what most people do. And they also have small bags for tips, so maybe if you only ate tortillas, food or drink you can get off with just a few coins and it will be ok.

And, to go back to the meaning, I think it's true. I think it's very slippery and difficult, we are moving in many waters when talking about indigenous groups. I don't think the anthropologist should feel bad about the fact that these groups are "disappearing", I think that's one subject we should discuss. How should we be talking about these people, calling them indigenous group or maybe using some other kind of name? So that's a serious problem.

Public 7: I guess the word indigenous is another one of indigenous like authenticity will be kind of. We no longer use the word limited to…

Imberton Deneke: Authenticity always goes back to aspects like origin, to the essentialist ideas. We have to get out of that discussion.

Karashima: Nakatani-san any comment?

Nakatani: No.

Karashima: Ok, thank you so much, please join me to thank to the presentator.

We have 20 minute's break starting at 3:35.

1   López Santillán, Angela and Gustavo Marín Guardado, "Turismo, capitalismo y producción de los exótico: una perspectiva crítica para el estudio de la mercantilización del espacio y la cultura", *Revista Relaciones 123*, Verano 2010, Vol. XXXI, p. 219-258.

2   This region, including the city of San Cristóbal and 17 rural municipalities (mostly indigenous), is now known as the Highlands of Chiapas.

3   Viqueira, Juan Pedro, "Historia crítica de los barrios de Ciudad Real", in Camacho, Dolores, Arturo Lomelí and Paulino Hernández coords., *La ciudad de San Cristóbal de Las Casas, a sus 476 años: una mirada desde las ciencias sociales*. Mexico: Gobierno del Estado de Chiapas, 2007.

4   Aguirre Beltrán, Gonzalo, *Formas de gobierno indígena*, Mexico: Instituto Nacional Indigenista, 1981 [1953].

5   Viqueira, Juan Pedro, 1995, "Los Altos de Chiapas. Una introducción general", in Viqueira, Juan Pedro and Mario Humberto Ruz ed., *Chiapas. Los rumbos de otra historia*, México: UNAM, CIESAS, CEMCA and Universidad de Guadalajara.

6   Viqueira, 2007, Op.cit; Aguirre Beltrán, 1981, Op. Cit.; Hvostoff, Sophie, "La comunidad abandonada. La invención de una nueva indianidad urbana en las zonas periféricas tzotziles y tzeltales de San Cristóbal de Las Casas, Chiapas, México (1974-2001) ", in Marco Estrada ed., *Chiapas después de la tormenta. Estudios sobre economía, sociedad y política*, Mexico: COLMEX, Gobierno del Estado de Chiapas y Cámara de Diputados LX Legislatura, 2009.

7   Pineda, Luz Olivia, "Del aeródromo al aeropuerto: larga batalla por abrirse al mundo", in Camacho, Dolores, Arturo Lomelí and Paulino Hernández coords., *La ciudad de San Cristóbal de Las Casas: a sus 476 años. Una mirada desde las ciencias sociales*, Mexico: Gobierno del Estado de Chiapas, Tuxtla Gutiérrez, 2007.

8   Rus, Jan, "La nueva ciudad maya en el valle de Jovel: urbanización acelerada, juventud indígena y comunidad en San Cristóbal de las Casas", in Marco Estrada ed., *Chiapas después de la tormenta. Estudios sobre economía, sociedad y política*, Mexico: COLMEX, Gobierno del Estado de Chiapas y Cámara de Diputados LX Legislatura, 2009. Viqueira, Juan Pedro, "Cuando no florecen las ciudades: la urbanización tardía e insuficiente de Chiapas", *Ciudades mexicanas del siglo XX: siete estudios históricos*, Mexico: El Colegio de México, Universidad Autónoma Metropolitana-Azcapotzalco, 2009.

9   Favre, Henri, *Cambio y continuidad entre los mayas de México*, Mexico: Instituto Nacional Indigenista, Colección INI Número 69, 1984.

10 Rus, Jan, 2009, Op-cit., pp.173-178.

11 I take this information from psychologist Patricia Greenfield (2009), who conducted research in Navenchauc in the 1970s and 1990s, tracing how weaving knowledge was transmitted from mother to daughter. She was part of the Harvard Chiapas project.

12 "Assignments" are part of the piece rate system in which the producer is paid per piece or unit made.

13 The NII's office in San Cristóbal started out in 1952, although the promotion of crafts seems to have begun in the 1970s.

14 Rus, Diana, "La crisis económica y la mujer indígena, caso Chamula", *INAREMAC*, Mexico: San Cristóbal de Las Casas, 1990.

15 Rus, Jan, "Una relectura de la etnografía tzotzil: la antropología y la política en Los Altos de Chiapas", 1955-2000, *Anuario*, San Cristóbal/Tuxtla Gutiérrez, Chiapas: Centro de Estudios Superiores de México and Centroamérica, Universidad de Artes y Ciencias de Chiapas, 2010, pp. 337-369.

16 Turok, Marta, 1976, "Diseño y símbolo en el huipil ceremonial de Magdalenas", *Boletín No.3*, Mexico: Departamento de Investigaciones de las Tradiciones Populares, 3 SEP, 1976.

17 There is no clear number of expellees (or refugees) arriving in the city, but we can trace a change in the number and social composition of its inhabitants. In 1990, the San Cristobal's population was 90,000 and 20,000 were indigenous people. In 2000, population was 120,000 and 60,000 indigenous (2009: 181-182).

18 Cañas Cuevas, Sandra, *Multiculturalismo mágico en una ciudad de Chiapas*, Mexico: Centro de investigaciones Multidisciplinarias sobre Chiapas y la Frontera Sur and Universidad Nacional Autónoma de México, 2017. Garza Tovar, Josué Roberto and Álvaro Sánchez Crispín, "Estructura territorial del turismo en San Cristóbal de Las Casas, Chiapas, México", *Cuadernos de Turismo*, no. 35, Universidad de Murcia, 2015, pp. 185-209,. ISSN: 1139-7861 e ISSN: 1989-4635 DOI: 10.6018/turismo.35.221571 (En línea, consultado 5 sept. 2017)

19 Nakatani, Ayami ed., *Fashionable Traditions: Asian Handmade Textiles in Motion*, Washington DC: Lexington, 2020, p.1.

20 Miyawaki, Chie, "'New Style' of Ethnic Clothing: Dress between Tradition and Fashion among the Hmong in Yunnan, China," in Ayami Nakatani ed., *Fashionable Traditions: Asian Handmade Textiles in Motion*, Washington DC: Lexington, 2020.

21 Center for Ainu & Indigenous Studies, Hokkaido University, *Living Conditions and Consciousness of Present-day Ainu: Report on the 2008 Hokkaido Ainu Living Conditions Survey*, 2010, p.3.

22 Morris-Suzuki, Tessa, "Performing Ethnic Harmony: The Japanese Government's Plans for

a New Ainu Law," *The Asia-Pacific Journal: Japan Focus*, Vol. 16 , Issue 21, No. 2, 2018, p.1.

23 Ibid., p.2.

24 Comment by Tahara Ryoko, cited in Morris-Suzuki, 2018, p.2.

25 Sayuri Umeda, "Japan: New Ainu law becomes effective," *Global Legal Monitor*, Library of Congress, Aug 5, 2019.

26 "Spirit of Ainu Handwork," a leaflet published by Biratori Town Office.

27 *Utsukushii Kimono (Beautiful kimonos)*, No. 269, Hearst Fujin Gaho, 2019, pp.146-153.

28 Nakatani, Ayami, "Listing Culures: Politics of Boundaries and Heritagization of Handwoven Textiles in Indonesia," in Ayami Nakatani ed., *Fashionable Traditions: Asian Handmade Textiles in Motion*, Washington DC: Lexington, 2020, pp.79-98.

移動する／文化交差的記憶のマテリアリズム

商品としてのテキスタイルに内在する記憶とは？

　第2部「移動する / 文化交差的記憶のマテリアリズム」では、商品化するテキスタイルの技術とデザインの具体的な事象の考察をもとに、絶え間ない移動のなかで人々がモノに見出そうとする記憶について議論が交わされた。テキスタイルは、衣服として身体を覆ったり隠したりする基本的な機能とともに、社会環境のなかで表現記号ともなる。その制作工程は本来、植物繊維の太さや長さを調節したり染色をしたりしてから糸を紡ぎ、経糸と緯糸を組み合わせて機にかけるという、手間のかかる作業だ。技術あるいはデザイン面におけるその特徴から、テキスタイルはある特定の文化の伝統的産物としてしばしば認識される。人類学や歴史学の過去を振り返ってみても織物の特徴を通してある文化の真正性を理解しようとする研究は決して少なくない。一方、市場経済のなかにおいて商品化されるテキスタイルは、手作業であれ機械制作であれ、その有用性が交換価値に変換され、モノとしてそれ自体に価値が付加される。服飾産業や観光産業はそれを民芸品として商品化したり一部のデザインを模倣して再生産したりしてテキスタイルを物象化する、まさにその現場となっている。そして、こうした動きは工芸推進などとして国家プロジェクトとしても生じている。このような状況、つまりテキスタイルが商品（モノ）として消費と生産の枠組みの中で流通し、同時に民族の集団的アイデンティティの表象としても機能することが期待されるというメカニズムのなかで、はたしてモノは記憶を内在しうるのだろうか。またその記憶とはどんな関係性のなかで織り込まれたものなのか。これらの問いについて二人の登壇者、グラシア・インベルトン・デネケ（発表者）と中谷文美（コメンテーター）が意見を交わし、さらに来館者からも反響的な声があがった。

変容を記憶するテキスタイル

　インベルトン・デネケは、自らの拠点とするメキシコのチアパス州サンクリストバル・デ・ラスカサスおよびその周辺、特にチアパス高地の先住民コミュニティにおいて、二十世紀後半にテキスタイルがどんな社会的アクターの手によって、どのように扱われてきたのかを明らかにすることで、伝統的民芸品としての織物への理解を再考することを試みる。現在わたしたちが手にするテキスタイルのどれにも民族アイデンティティの記憶が不変的に保存されていると考えるのはあまりにも安易だろう。時代を経る過程においてテキスタイルにはその制作方法と使用方法、両者に間違いなく多様でダイナミックな変化が生じてきた。言い換えれば、織物に編み込まれた記憶は変容のそれである。チアパスの織物は、チアパスという特定の地域における特定の歴史的なモーメントがその都度要求する社会条件に適合することによって、その様相を変化させてきた。植民地時代まで遡ってみれば現在の在り方との差異は明らかだ。現サンクリストバル・デ・ラスカサスは植民地時代、1528 年にスペイン人の手によって建設された街であり、その周辺に住むインディオを管理する中枢であった。スペイン人が支配する世界のなかにあって、インディオたちは労働力として奉仕することが求められた。そして彼らが纏う織物は、属するコミュニティを分別するための記号として機能し、スペイン人による監視および管理を容易にする道具となった。

　20 世紀後半に焦点を絞って考察してみると、テキスタイルがまさに躍動的な変容を求められてきた過程を知ることができる。インベルトン・デネケは経済的社会状況と多方面からの社会的アクターの介入に言及しながら、その変容の過程を提示する。農業危機と商業的民芸品生産の必要性、工芸技術の国家による推進事業、農村部から都市への大量移住、観光ブームの到来。状況を大枠に区分することで、それぞれの場面で社会的アクターがどのように機能したのかを明確にしようとした。簡潔にはなるが、順に追ってみよう。

　チアパス高地農村部の先住民は、20 世紀の半ばまで低地にあるプランテーションやアシエンダで働くことによって生業を立ててきた。低地の農地所有者との間を手配師が斡旋し、高地の労働者はトウモロコシやフリホーレスの栽培、後半にはコーヒー農園へも派遣され、それによってわずかばかりの収入を得た。

当時、チアパス高地の先住民がサンクリストバルで売り物にしたものといえば、農産物や薪、炭、そして塩。織物はあくまで家族が使用する範囲で制作された。そして織物の制作にあたって、作り手には自らの手で牧畜を営めるほどの経済的余裕がなかったため、素材となる羊毛も市場に依存していた。けれども 1970 年代後半から 80 年代にかけてメキシコ全土で農業危機が起こる。農業だけではもはや生活が成り立たなくなり、大規模な人口の増加とも相まって経済状況の変化が求められた。こうした環境のなかで先住民の家計の一旦を担い始めるのが織物製品だったのだ。というのも、サンクリストバルに滞在する旅行客や人類学者が彼らの纏う衣服、特にウイピルやレボソに興味を示し、店舗経営者が先住民女性と契約関係を築き始めたからだ。この契約関係は対等なものだったとは言い難い。当時の状況を表す具体例として、インベルトンはナベンチャウック村を挙げる。その村の職人はときに大量の織物製品を短時間で生産することが要求された。そして要求を満たすため職人の間に組織立った結びつきが生まれ、それを取り仕切る代表者も出現する。この結果、一つの先住民コミュニティの中で、組織を仕切る代表者とそれ以外の織物職人との間で経済的な差が生じ始める。前者はサンクリストバルの店舗経営者や外国からやってくる商人と懇意になり、後者は職人として織物に付加される価値について知らされないままに生産に携わり続けたからだ。また、生産物自体も購入者側のニーズに適合するように形を変えていく。クッションカバーやテーブル掛けなどはこの時期に生産が増えていった製品と言える。

　これに並行して、国家機関や国外の人類学者など外部の権威者たちによって、テキスタイルを含めた先住民コミュニティの工芸が真正な伝統を継承するシンボリックなモノとして解釈されるようになる。一方では、メキシコ政府が先住民を国家の一員として「教育」し、メスティソ社会に組み込むため農村部の近代化政策を打ち出す。この国民統合政策では、インディヘニスモの一環として、先住民コミュニティにおける民芸生産技術の保存と向上が推進された。民芸品制作を促進することで、都心部への大量移住による農村部の過疎化を抑えること、同時に観光産業の発展に寄与することが期待されたのだ。また他方で、ハーヴァード大学の人類学者を中心とした研究プロジェクトチームがチアパス高地を調査のため訪問するのもこの頃のことだ。彼らの多くは現存する先住民文

化に古代マヤとの連続性を探求し、その本質主義的な観点からテキスタイルに
シンボリックな解釈を試みたのだった。これら二つの権威的グループは、先住
民コミュニティのエスニシティを誇張しながら、その織物に真正的な伝統工芸
品なる語りを付与し、増強したと言える。

　さらに言えば、サンクリストバルで人とモノの移動が盛んになったことも考
慮しなければならない。一つに、民芸職人として生計を立てることが難しかっ
た者、あるいは政治的、宗教的対立によってコミュニティから追放された者が、
都市へ職を求めて移住する。すると都市の中でもともとサンクリストバル市民
であった者と先住民移住者間との対立が生じた。この対立は民芸品を売る露店
や店舗がどこに配置されるかという都市空間の問題に大きく関与した。そして
もう一つに、観光客の出現があげられる。70年代後半から国際的な規模で「発
展途上国」の観光開発が推進され、サンクリストバルはその地理的歴史的条
件から観光地として整えられる。また1994年のサパティスタの蜂起によって、
ジャーナリストや研究者、アクティヴィストの注目も集め、街は人とモノの移
動の中心として機能するようになった。

　以上の具体的な事象を踏まえてインベルトン・デネケはこう結論づける。商
品（モノ）としてのテキスタイルには、チアパス高地の先住民が直面した生活
環境の変化が記憶として編み込まれている。移動と交換の絶え間ない市場メカ
ニズムの中でその記憶は再生産され続ける。

生産者とモノの近接

　これに対して中谷は、生産者が個人レベルで抱くであろう、テキスタイルを
含めた伝統民芸品そして伝統服飾品との感情的な結びつきを考慮した問いを投
げかける。生産過程における技術や素材、作業形態、あるいはテキスタイルを
身につける際の作法や習慣は、外部の目からすれば大きく変化したように見え
る。なかには、「伝統的」領域とは一線を画した一見コスプレと見紛うような
着こなしもある。けれど生産者であり同時に消費者でもある先住民にとって、
それはエスニシティ表象のなかで形成された「新しさ」なのではないか。その
ように考えたとき、「真正性」とは一体何をもって判断されうるものであるのか。
中谷は生活習慣の変容に伴って着こなしや用いられ方が変化を遂げたとしても、

そこには変わらず民族の集団的アイデンティティを見出しうるのではないかと問う。それは中谷自身が文化的近接（cultural proximity）と呼ぶ、市場向けの生産物であれ、自らが身につけるための生産であれ、生産者と生産物との間に生じているはずの結びつきのことだ。

　以上の問いをより明確にするため、中谷はアイヌが直面する先住民としての権利やアイデンティティの問題に言及する。同化政策のもとで制定された「旧土人保護法」が 1997 年になってやっと廃止され、「アイヌ文化振興法」が成立した。しかし、先住民としての権利保障は、2019 年の新法まで待たなければならない。ただし、この法律でも土地や漁業権などの権利回復は盛り込まれていない。法的な整備が不十分ななか、他方でアイヌ文化は国の観光産業としてますます重要視されつつある。旧アイヌ民族博物館は国立博物館「民族共生空間ウポポイ」としてリニューアルされ、2020 年に予定されていたオリンピック開幕にあわせて開館された。また国が定める伝統的工芸品産業のなかに、アイヌの工芸品アットゥシとサラニプが指定されている。これは産地の人々にとっての悲願ではあったが、他方で差別や権利の問題が解決されないままに文化振興だけが一人歩きする側面もある。民芸品の技術やデザインの魅力のみに注目を集め、文化振興のもとで聞こえてくる語りは、はたしてアイヌとして生きる人々のアイデンティティの問題を含んだものになっているだろうか。中谷は、文化振興や商品化によって生産物と生産者の間の結びつきが希薄する現状にこそ、工芸品というモノに生産者自身が受け継いできた記憶を見出そうと試みるべきではないのだろうか、と提案する。

　二人の発表は、テキスタイルというモノをそれぞれ異なる視点から考察する試みと捉えることができる。けれども、両者はともに一つの大きな関心事を前提に理解される必要があるだろう。本文を閉じる前に、その問いに触れる必要がある。それは、先住民とは一体だれのことを指すのか、という問いだ。先住民とは、だれと区別されるための呼び名なのか。他のだれとの関わりのなかで産み出されてきたのか。その「だれ」は、チアパス高地のツォツィルやツェルタルや他の先住民にとってはコンキスタドールであり、後にメキシコ政府や北米の人類学者、あるいは観光客にとって変わられた。そしてアイヌにとっては、中谷の発表に限って言えば日本という想像的共同体がそれにあたる。二人の発

表者は、「彼ら」が支配と収奪の対象として客体化される過程で、先住民という他者として識別され、一つの民族であることを否応なく認識せざるを得なかった事実を物語るモノとしてテキスタイルを扱い、同時に、資本主義社会で商品化＝モノ化される過程を通して、その事実が形骸化している様を提示した。研究者としての利己的な事案に傾倒することなく、わたしたちは作り手である先住民に目を向けて議論ができているか。この問いは来館者の一人から投げかけられたものだ。研究者としての関心事はどこに向いていて、モノを通して人間社会のどんな問題を理解しようとしているのか。生産物としてのモノは人との関係性のなかで存在する。第2部は、余りにも必然的となったこの問いを振り返り、再考する場となった。（鋤柄史子）

Part 3

—

The Materiality of Words
and Archive

Part 3

The Materiality of Words and Archive

Hiroki Ogasawara: Ok, we have just one hour to go, to the end of the wonderful day. I suppose particularly those people who are sitting in front of you, they must have been tired by now. I think this conclusive session must be an open one, flexible one, so at any moment if you want to say something, raise your hand. As I told you this morning, your intervention is always welcome. Then in this program, I'll pass microphone to Fumiko first. Fumiko Sukikara, she graduated from the faculty of intercultural studies many, many years ago. I don't remember exactly when you were my student anyway. So she is wondering around all of the world, including Kiyose in Tokyo, Barcelona and Mexico. Then for some reason she ended up in San Cristobal de Las Casas to get another MA, actually it's your second MA, master degree. Wonderful person she is. She likes studying. I'm telling you, my students, she likes studying. So she is going to give some comments, maybe few questions to them. The second person who speaks is Koko Nango, here, a research fellow in PROMIS, our center. Then, as I told you this morning she had a kind few months in San Cristobal de Las Casas with help of Gracia, and Fumiko and other staffs of the Autonomous University of Chiapas. And she has some comments and she has got her own small topic, one topic, something to do with folklore studies. Then all of you, maybe you can respond to comments provided by these young scholars. Right, if you're all ready, go ahead please.

Fumiko Sukikara
Word and Materiality
Fumiko Sukikara: First of all, I really would like to express my thanks to all of

you; to Gracia and José Luis for coming, and to Hiroki for inviting us here. I'll share with you the ideas which I had in listening to the two previous sessions.

Archive as Memories Which Turned into Objects

I think archiving memories can be understood preserving the past in an orderly way and in a certain unit. Archiving is also the operation of materializing memories, that is, converting memories into things. For example, the museums or archaeological ruins about which José Luis spoke are symbolic places of the materialized pasts. In those spaces the selected artifacts are gathered and placed in order. As Gracia told us, the Chiapas textiles became commodified, at the same time started to be identified as symbol of the Mayan peoples' "authentic" memories.

In addition, the words also have been materialized. As Walter Ong discussed in his book, the written words are detached from their oral nature, from the ability to flow freely in air, and are put into visible form in books. The words were fixed in a world of visual space by printing.

In this sense, materializing is also understood as making things visible. The technique of visualization has given a powerful impact to all the dimensions of our life, as the photographic history tells us. The photography makes it possible to demonstrate a past, cutting one scene from the whole and focusing through a certain angle. And these visual images turned into a part of an archive: an archive of memories that permanently preserves a moment of that time, by which we recall experiences and sensations we would have. Likewise, the maps are also a powerful visual representation technique. The map gives us a spatial understanding based on some concepts and conditions. In its representation, thematic aspects such as the political division of land or the demographic characteristics are recorded in a summarized way, and in this sense, the map is the device for archiving the historical events as well.

However, the more important thing here is that, as José Luis and Gracia told us, the archived pasts are represented in different ways and through different narratives and techniques. The history of the Czech museum is a significant example. José Luis' talk also made me think a lot about the dilemma of working with materials originally coming from a faraway time from us. Anthropologists and historians or any others, who seek to interpret pasts, situate themselves between the two spatially and timely different worlds: between their own present and the other that is narrated in the archive. And depending on its objective and method of how to approach it, the past appears with a different face.

Gracia showed us how the textiles have been woven with various memories by different operators over the centuries in Los Altos de Chiapas; and so that, into textiles the different meanings have been inserted. For the Spaniards they were signs to distinguish the "types" of the Indians; After the revolution the national institutes sought to emphasize in them the "traditional" characteristics in order to include them in part of the cultural patrimony of Mexico; and some anthropologists and intellectuals reinterpret them according to the discourse of the symbolic value, by means of which they used to contemplate continuity with the indigenous past. I'm convinced of Gracia's words that we find in textiles the memories of interpretations.

How to Preserve and Reproduce the Past? In Which Technique and in Which Language?

From here I would like to share with you the reflections on the theme connecting with my own experiences. I start with the following questions: how the past has been preserved and reproduced? In which technique and in which language?

These questions arose to me from two stories related to the restoration. One story is about the site of Teotihuacan, which locates close to Mexico City. José Luis told me this story when we were together in a cantina in San Cristobel de Las Casas. When restoring the stairs of some old buildings in this ruin, the persons in charge of the archaeological project added more steps than those which they actually recognized. This technique of reproduction, namely the complementing, has been used in several other places. For example, Bonampak. This is one of the archaeological zones located on the border of Guatemala and Mexico. while restoring this spot, they put the various vivid colors on monochrome mural, which had been decayed by time and lost their tone. Likewise, some ancient paintings are restored in various times with new materials and renovated techniques. They are the cases of the complementing technique: add something more to what has been left in the present.

On the other hand, there is another reproduction technique; it is to exclude a fragment of what had remained until that moment. Another story about restoration will help me describe this technique. With a restorer friend, one of my friends who studies restoration, I went to listen to a lecture about the agents involved in preservation and restoration. One of the speakers, who have worked in urban space as a restorer, put on the table a discussion about graffiti artists and their works, and asked, "Aren't graffiti on murals of buildings in the city the memories to preserve? On the one hand, the old buildings, which were constructed at colonial times in the historic center of Mexico City, are considered historically valuable and protected by international law. In the same way, the cave paintings in Baja California, considered thousands of years old' art drawn by "our ancestors" are carefully preserved. On the other hand, the graffiti painted on city buildings are erased without consideration. Interestingly, however, it seems that among the graffiti artists there is an agreement on how to evaluate their paintings; the special pieces do not clean and leave them in the same place for a long time, while there are graffities that disappear immediately and on them others paint new one.

This discussion about graffities in urban space makes me think about what kind of the pasts is the subject of preserving, archiving and restoring; for and by whom some are defined as the past worth archiving and others not; and from what moment do they turned into memorable past for us. It's possible to say that the past moments are always interpreted, signified and hierarchized, always from the future point of view. And some materials like graffiti, in spite of being historical fragments, have been cleaned and covered as if they would not exist ever. That have caused because of the hierarchization of pasts.

In this sense, it may also need to ask: In which language we reproduce memories? Some anthropologists have considered the Chiapas textiles as a representation of the authentic elements or the techniques traditionally transmitted among the indigenous people. And "Mexicanity" as José Luis has told us, is a case of the language used for involving indigenous peoples in the nation-state. Graffities are, in other hand, largely erased by the discourse of urban landscape preservation.

The Word 'Maya' as A Space for Archiving and Device of Reproduction

Now I would like to focus specifically on the question of languages and words, which is more related to my study. the word itself can be understood as storage of meanings and signs, and at the same time as device of reproduction. When we use a word, its previous histories resonate each other in our mind. The storage room opens and causes us to imagine the ideas stored in the word. We can think about it with the word "Maya". This word would imply many concepts; civilization, antiquity, ethnicity, cosmovision, mysterious world, man of the corn, the end of the world, textiles etc. Those concepts are related to the word "Maya", to the extent that we historically and socially have studied and tried to understand Maya as a part of our world. What we imagine when hearing or reading "Mayan textiles", "Mayan civilization", or "secret Mayan jungle"? Obviously, these ideas are not intrinsic in their own nature, but are historically constructed and developed.

When interpreting a word or a series of words –texts–, we consciously or unconsciously recognize in it a meaning pertinent to the current condition, selecting ones among those applied. Through the act of interpretation, it sometimes may cause to romanticize the previous stories or at other times to invent a totally new meaning. Thus, the word Maya has acquired every instant a new validity, taking on a new meaning. This, for example, has happened when the Maya for the first time became an object of study among Western intellectuals; when it has been a major scene in science fiction films or novels; and when it has been regarded as a powerful and inspiring art as well as the "primitive" arts of Africa. In this sense, the science is a simple part of the production and reproduction of the Maya, as José Luis says. Both the dynamics of the mercantile products –textiles and huipiles–, as well as the Hollywood films collaborate in dimension this process of construction. All ideas are in a chain of interpretation. For, the interpretation, following the sociologist George Steiner, can be understood as an act that gives life to languages beyond the place and the moment of its immediate enunciation or transcription.

This is my comment. Thank you.

Ogasawara: The past is created by the future point. So let´s do, Koko.

Koko Nango
Classics, Canons and Materiality
Koko Nango: I am very happy to attend this event with Gracia, José Luis, Fumiko. This day is special for me. Thank you, Ogasawara Sensei.

I research Japanese old stories, many of which have roots in narratives. Without "frozen and framing", in Fumiko's phrase, such old stories would disappear. Without frozen by letters, printing or digital technics we couldn't access lots of old stories. And needless to say, people kept trying not to disappear stories. Stories were written, translated, and printed, therefore we can access the world of the old stories. But if anyone does not read, the frozen stories keep frozen. Now as for my comment, I want to introduce a case of technology and memories at the point of Japanese classic literature that is my major.

In Japan the technology of printing was gotten from China in the 8th century. And it was the 17th century when people start to use the technology in ordinal. By the technology many people in Japan could get to read classic books like *Kojiki*, *Nihonshoki*, or *Genjimonogatari* and so on. Before spreading printing technology such classic books had been written as manuscripts and people could access such books had been limited.

But by the technology many old and special books could be accessed easily by people who could read letters and character in the days. And the contents of the classic books that had kept to be special knowledge became well-known widely.

That is, the technological innovation on the books led to change "Japanese culture". In Edo period many "traditions" were reborn, which came to be known through the printed books.

And with modernization in 19th century new change of letters had started. Now this is a printing book, *Isemonogatari* [Figure 1]. And this is also *Isemonogatari* [Figure 2]. This one is manuscript. The connected letters in both Figures are called KUZUSHIJI; letters written in a cursive style.

This is a board for printing [Figure 3], that isn't for *Isemonogatari*, just for reference. For printing, the board is painted black and covered by a piece of paper. And the letters are transferred from the board to the paper.

And now we have many such printing books and manuscripts as materials in libraries or museums which have the faculties as archives in Japan. And by progressing digital technology now we can access those books as materials, but not memories.

Most people can't read such letters nowadays. We can read only letters separated each other. The phrase written in [Figure1] and [Figure 2] is like this "Mukashi otoko arikeri. Himugashi no Gojo watari ni ito shinobite ikikeri". The meaning is as follows. "Once upon a time, there was a man. He went to around the east of the Gojo to meet his lover, in secretly." But today, most of us can't read such connecting letters. Letters need to be separated now because we use books printed from type set. Japanese government adopted such type printing for school textbook in modernization and westernization of Japan. As a result, such letters are discarded.

The environment around letters keeps changing roughly, with the changing time. It is fact that many books as materials have been in archives. But the memories can't stand up vividly. Some researchers insist students need to study how to read such character and letters3. And the AI for reading such letters is developing rapidly. But on the other hand, now in Japan, people start to argue about the necessity of the studying classic literature itself. They say it is too difficult for students to study and it is not useful. I am afraid the classic literature will become something for some devotees or researchers. It may not be distant future the specialist is needed to understand the contents of the past books and mediate the materials and readers. As is the letters themselves, we will be separated from old stories. It is fact archives are constructing and blushing up. But at the same time, the talent of understanding the contents are losing now.

Stories can be active by listening, speaking and reading. Without them books are only objects. Now in Japan classic books are getting objects. Those would be vivid when specialists mediate people and books like tourist guide.

This is my comment. I think this is related with your presentation, this is the Japanese recent case and I wonder, how is the situation concerning memories and archives. Thank you.

Round Table Discussion

Ogasawara: Thank you. Her question is regarding the recent kind of corrupt humanities and social sciences. They want corrupt access by them whoever you need. They want corrupt access because these staffs are useless; it's not pragmatic, they say. It's one thing in wasting money and human resources, in wasting civilisation, not like, for example, genetics, medical sciences and other natural sciences; it's not even basic research, neither applied sciences too. What's required in this country is those staffs who can produce global human resource as well as money. But we here together today, we are just wasting time, I'm sorry about this. But it's really important.

For example, Fumiko's point, the past is created in a way produced by the future; in the sense that actually we don't have ideas as to what was happening in the past but we set out perspectives to asking about the past, by choosing appropriate languages, by choosing appropriate perspectives, by doing etc.. So this might be the past but we don't understand what it wrote. So we may ask her, Koko, what does it say? Then she can show us this character. It does say a meaning like this, but it's not saying exactly what it is about. That' why I choose this subject matter of our conference: Materialism of Archive. くずし字, or 草書, hand-written character, or 楷書, typed character, we can all understand them. It does say this but the content might be the same, or as a material they are totally different. But it was written 1000 years ago, by Kino Tsurayuki, so that one is supposed to be a thing of the past; Kino Tsurayuki wrote it in the year of 900 or something. Even not in this manner, this is the copy. So it's kind of the entrance gate to reach at the very original source of something that must have happened. We never know. So that's why we have to create a path, a path road to ask about this kind of material. But in these processes we need to invent or fabricate, re-institutionalise or restore some, artificial controllers, manoeuvre things that we want to know. So that is the kind of summary of your papers. Then I pass my microphone to José Luis, Gianluca, Gracia and Ayami, you may have some comments. Not only for comments or questions but, the reflexion of all sessions.

Escalona Victoria: It's interesting how we get involved in some fields and issues of interest for science, and how we keep involved in them a for long time. We learn and even recreate specialties, fields of study for very specific objects, like the language and the writing systems. It's quite interesting, too, how we change those disciplines and how we use new technologies, like photography for example, to visualize and understand the remains of our past in new ways, recreating the past as well. And I think the real problem for students like us, is to recognize that we are permanently in the processes of making knowledge. Sometimes, I have this discussion with historians. In some ways, historians are very clear about it, because they try to understand the past by reading documents, and they accept that documents are a faulty evidence of the past, in different levels. That is true because we could have three or four sources to contrast, and sometime these are not concurrent about the facts. But the solution is not to discard the query, but to look for more evidence. You can go even deeply as well into the making process of these documents or material remains, asking for how they were made, in which language, how we are able to read them currently, and so on. We start having problems as soon as we go throughout these questions. And it happens very often, and knowledge can change in tiny shares, modifying our present interpretations, but it happen in a cumulative way to the point that, eventually, research could drive the whole reinterpretation, to a new revolutionary view of our past.

Ogasawara: Thank you. Sometimes we are really afraid of representing something. In the age of political correctness, the subaltern functions and whatsoever, but we do speak, on behalf of something, on behalf of something represented. Sometimes, maybe 20 years ago or 25 years ago a lot of discussions about the limits of representation, impossibility of representation took place. Some of them can speak, and unless we are not subalterns we can speak. They can speak, we can speak, who can speak? The discussion is going on but too many restrictions, too much political correctness, it is indeed important, significant that we have to really do political correctness, to answer in politically correct manner, behaviour whatever; sometime too much, you know. Yes. So Gianluca.

Gatta: My comment is less analytical than evocative. I would like to tell you a story that encompass some keywords of today's discussions. In the last speeches, both Fumiko and Koko talked about language and narrative. Today, we started from objects and we arrived at more dialogical issues.

The story I am going to tell perfectly fits this circularity, i.e. the intertwining of materiality and narration. I would like to talk about the object in [Figure 4]. In the 80s, a small archive of diaries was opened in a small town in Tuscany[1]. So, we have a small town, a small archive, a very peripheral area. The aim of this archive was to collect diaries: self-narrations by common people, very often written in vernacular language. When we think of diaries, we usually think of paper, if anything handwritten paper. But in 1986, Clelia Marchi, a 72-year-old country woman left, maybe for the first time, her small village. She took a train, then a bus, and reached the town where the archive was located. Once there, she walked up to the archive's door holding a package: "are you the archive of diaries?", she asked those in charge, "I have something for you." At first sight, they thought it was a present, maybe some food from the countryside. Not at all, it was a bed sheet, upon which she had written her story. She had lost her husband some months before and one night she felt a compelling desire to write her story. But she could not find any pieces of paper in her home. So, she thought: "ancient people used to envelope their relatives' corpses into bed sheet. Since I can't use it anymore with my husband in my everyday life, I can use it for my story." The title of her self-narration is "Not even a lie", as if to say "this is my truth!". She also put Jesus Christ, some symbolic ritual things, and her husband's picture on the canvas. The first words of her diary are, I roughly translate: "Dear people, please treasure this bed sheet, because it saves a little bit of my life, of my husband. Clelia Marchi, 72 years-old, wrote the story of her land's people by filling up a bed sheet with writings, from farming work to affects." So, a totality of a life-world has been transformed into a material object very different from a classic paper diary. There is a sort of aesthetic gesture in this spontaneous materialization of memory, which had not been "triggered" by any anthropologist. The historians and anthropologists involved in the archiving and dissemination of her story acted just as a "listening contexts". There is a difference in this: anthropologists gathering vs. anthropologists listening, and also waiting for something to happen around them, just staying there and collecting this kind of autonomous voices. I think Clelia Marchi's subjectification is a good example of how materiality, narration, subjectivity, objectivation work in everyday life, putting together language, narrative, aesthetic, and the narrative/listening process. This written bed sheet became the symbol of the museum, it has been located in a central space, it has been hierarchized, it is the top of this museum, but maybe it was worth doing that. I think this was an evocative story to sum up many of the issues that we discussed today. And particularly, it shows how things not only can divert from their path to becoming commodities, in Appadurai's terms[2], but also how they can divert from their everyday life use into more symbolic, ritual use, out of everyday life. Thank you.

Ogasawara: Thank you. Also commemoration takes place here. Not only intimate relationship with her and her husband but also with display like this whenever you step on in this room you could see narratives, stories, you could see the life of this old lady as well as her own narrative, not just herself but her narrative, too.

Gatta: And the process and the materials too. What do the materials add to the story? Maybe this is the question.

Ogasawara: Well. Thank you, good to think like this. Gracia, ready?

Imberton Deneke: Well I only have a small comment actually. But listening to Ayami talking about Ainu, maybe think about how similar thing she described form very far away country from Mexico, how similar the situation she describes where to I have seen. And I go back to question, are they really similar or using only this anthropological perspective finding common case; indigenous, authenticity. I think these things are real things there. It happens that the national states create narratives and anthropologist create narratives, but for those who are students and also who are still working on this search project I think it's important to break away or come away from this perspective, and try to find other ways to reach these things. We could be talking about same place with same words, and maybe it's not, we shouldn't do only that. That is there it's common, you know we share everything but probably we just using like stencil. So I'm happy to conference here because I can be aware of it. Thank you.

Nakatani: I want to go back to the issue of textiles. Being anthropologist, I do not study textiles just as materials or objects; rather, they represent the materialization of various, on-going forces and interests. There may be political relations between the producers, dealers, and consumers. There may be a political agenda behind these textiles to keep a certain boundary intact, or there may be economic interests for providing local women with additional income. There may be a universal discourse on cultural heritage involved.

Also, textiles travel across time, space and cultural boundaries. Gracia gave me this nice small bag. In my eyes, it is just a cute bag and I find its color scheme interesting. This same color combination may have a specific connotation for its producers in Chiapas; but at least they could make this bag only after they had access to artificial bright colors like this. This piece is open to interpretations and various types of understanding.

Another point about the relationship between archives and memories. As I said before, textiles are mobile and changeable in forms. At the same time, however, as Gracia may have mentioned in passing, a particular motif or a pattern can be archived in the surface of textiles. So, for the specific meaning of this symbol, for example, a bird or a flower or whatever, it's like fixation of a historical point going back to some legend or some episode or emblems in the past. In this sense, motifs can be archived.

But memories cannot be fixed. When we deal with both archive and memories, memories can be more open to interpretation.

Ogasawara: Thank you. Well we have another 15 or 20 minutes to go. I think we should take some opinions or questions. But yes, traveling. I want to mention about traveling. Translation, trans-culturalization, transfer, mobility and traveling. Things can travel.

But the question is, things can travel with human being, or things can travel by themselves, or things can travel from where to where? That is maybe to do with your final open questions. Well, another thing is, I'm a sociologist. You're anthropologists. I take the advantage of this age of political correctness or something, because you're brave enough to getting into the field, meet the people, listen to the people, getting some materials like you, historians. The historians are coming to the archive, checking the documents and everything, then file up. You (anthropologists) file up too. We, sociologists, snatch it. Then use it and theorize it from the very arrogant point of view. So it's kind of, we are thieves basically, in academic discipline's. You can come over anywhere according to your interest, according to desire to learn, desire to know, desire to study. But for some reason we are separated, compartmentalized into; like you're anthropologist, you're historian, you're political scientist, you're artist, you're singer, you're novelist. So I think we have to sometimes deliberately reject this compartmentalization. That is my emotional plea for those who attended here. So, any comments? Yes please.

Public 1: Thank you. First of all thank you for presentations and comments. I have maybe one question for Professor Nakatani, and also that question is for all of Japanese audiences. So it's interesting to see you show us like one business about Chinese traditional culture; because I'm Chinese by the way. You also have that question; said that, is it *cos-play* or just traditional cloth. And in my opinion, I think now those people, you should traditional cloth in a province. So as you mean, now in the inner it's very popular in tourist place like everyday they come to visit and come to inner province, they visit different place, and also can try to wear this kind of traditional cloth, but instead of go inner, so called traditional cloth but for me I would like just call now *cos-play* or costume like so. Because I know that in Japan there is a person; he or she wants to wear the kimono to join to attend the event in Shibuya. Is where to think that. He wears Kimono; the people around him, they're just like zombie or evil. That person wears the Kimono. In China we have this kind of event too and also there is a big event for gamers we call like "China Joys". People from all over the world they can wear Chinese traditional clothes like Kung-fu. So is it ok for people to wear like these cloth like everywhere. But in Japan, back to the question, do you think it's too sensitive or overactive because I don't know if you have the issue between Kyoto and Kim

Kardashian, because of the Kimono. Even the Mayor of Kyoto, he wrote later to Kim Kardashian to suggest to stop using this word because of this is all world sense. So that is my question to all, or it's too sensitive to deal with or come up the question. Thank you.

Ogasawara: キム・カーダシアンというモデルの人が下着のブランドを立ち上げたんですよ。そのブランド名が「キモノ」っていう。京都市長がですね、何で京都なのか、京都は何を代表しているつもりなのかわからんのですが、市長の門川さんが、ブランド名を取り下げろとかなんとか、訴訟するとかしないとか言い出した。どう思いますか。個人的に、ぼくはどうでもいいと思っているんですけど。そういうと話が終わっちゃうので。

Is it about Kimono as cloth or is it about Kimono as sign? And also a kind of traditional western perception of kimono is not right; (not) proper wear, it's more kind of 19th century or early 20th century Japonist, orientalist imagination of Kimono, like wardrobe, like yukata. Andy Warhol だって着てたんだし。I think some trench between those who are really critical to Kim Kardashian's suggestion and those who are not. Any other things, come on.

Nakatani: Can I say some words responding to him? The word *cos-play*, which I used in my description of an ethnic minority in Yunann, may not be particularly relevant. But what I wanted to argue was that the word *cos-play* can work in two different ways; it may mean the joy of radical style, a radical rapture from a traditional or conventional form, while appreciating the representation of identity. But on the other end of a spectrum, you can argue that their new style is not authentic, it's not traditional any more, because they have relinquished their conventional techniques, materials and all that; "what are you doing? It's just a *cos-play*," outsiders may say. And this goes back to the issue of kimono as well.

The kimono is already so detached from the majority of Japanese life-worlds. I can't wear kimono by myself, though I own some. My son probably has never touched any kimono until we stayed in Japanese-style *ryokan*. Yet kimono has been jealously guarded as Japanese tradition, and because of that, traditional techniques of making kimono have continued to survive so far all over Japan. But it's very small niche industry. Kimono cultures enforce many strict rules and by so doing, the practices surrounding kimono have been fossilized, and then alienated from the daily life of ordinary Japanese. It's a huge problem when it comes to a textile discourse in Japan. None of us, sitting here in this room, may not be familiar with kimono in the same way as *indigena* people of Chiapas or ethnic minorities in China are with their own traditional clothes. We are in a very different situation.

Ogasawara: Anybody else, please. Any historians?

Masato Karashima: I have a question but honestly my question is out of the content. But I'll say that. I am historian, economic historian, so I'm interested in infrastructure. Today we are talking about mobility so I have a question to Gracia. I guess the development of the transportation, specially highway or new airport or something like that, trigger the transportation, the stabilization of textile or tourism. May I ask? That is very basic question.

Imberton Deneke: Yes I think it relieve that and not only tourism now and in last 20 years; but even before the indigenous villages are very far away and the road to these places. And like in 70's or 80's in the case what we are talking now about, people there, some family have trucks because of one of these development problems, decided that people have need to transport or something. And they decided to go to Mexico City to buy yarn for textiles and weave that in San Cristobal. So I can imagine this people who very rare speak Spanish never have been out of there, basically in region they knew; not driving to Mexico City maybe like 25 hours or 30 hours bring back the top clothes and yarn they are getting there. So yes, the infrastructure is very important for all these changes and has been going on. And in this case there is other implication. Their bag is very large; yarn cane is very large. So they have to make small box to self to public. It's kind of using child labour to make this thing and children stop going to school because they have to make this. So many changes started from there. But the infrastructure is super important for all these changes.

Public 2: I also guess, in order to contain the Zapatista uprising the national government do some militaristic, some developmental policy in this region, I guess from outside of view. So some militaristic policy is developing some highway in order to centrum quick up, for example? And change the region in cultural or some (aspects).

Imberton Deneke: Well, yes the new road to new airport, and like military had waters all around Chiapas but there is a very important study in 20 years later, 2014, about the economic statistics of development in region. And it was in the same situation as before the Zapatista uprising. So basically little change happened then in those far as this economic statistics can tell. But many other things were radically changed.

Public 3: Thank you very much for stimulating discussion. I don't have any qualification to say something here, I arrived here just, I don't know, one hour ago. I really wanted to ask you several things, some of complicated, so I wanted to articulate what I am thinking now. First I was expecting to listen to your presentation in your, what is your language, in Spanish or in Japanese or in native language of course. And I was really wondering why you speak in English here. And what represent this situation. So maybe I think you're not personally connected to English speaking culture except for Ogasawara sensei.

Ogasawara: José Luis got PhD from Manchester.

Public 3: I'm sorry. I didn't know that. But this topic itself is how can be connected to the factor of speaking English. And this part is connected to my another question. I think the culture is very delicate and divers. And sometimes the elements cannot be translated into your cultural feel. I recently met one art-historian who is also anthropologist, whose major is Papua New Guinea's textile and he wanted to see some hidden textile inside of spiritual house. Basically this house is very exclusive; the outsider can't enter into the house. But eventually he could get enter there and he saw many brilliant textiles. Of course he didn't understand symbolism or meanings. But actually the textiles are repeated same motifs and he thought that there is some repetition of some symbolic style. He asked the local people, what does it mean. That local people answer to him, what is "it"? It's not it; they are thousand gods inside. And each pattern is different but for this Japanese anthropologist they're just one image, one repetition. But for local people it's very various patterns. One to for them it's one thousand. So what I want to say that you're speaking English here and we are thinking that we share something. But at the same time, we cannot get certain delicate element behind our conversation; it's kind of limitation of representation. How can we get be culturalized here or whether how any guilty to get deep. Sorry, it's some complicated question but.

Ogasawara: I can have a go but I let you speak first.

Escalona Victoria: It is another way to approach the problem of frames. English language works here also as frame, because I am not able to speak to you in Japanese (I am sorry about that) and it would be probably difficult to sustain our conversation in Spanish, because some of us do not speak Spanish. Thus, speaking in English, which is not for the most of us our mother language, has been the way to make possible this session. But, in any case, any language would work as frame, because whatever language we had decided use here, should worked in the same way. And even if we share the same language, we have the same problem, because every conversation implies certain level of translation.

I realized now that the whole encounter has been a fragmentary conversation that has been interweaved by every one of the participants, as accurately and artistically as possible. We are never going to get to the deepest end of the thing (it would be the end of the conversation). However, we are making new efforts, once again, to get the deepest as possible. And tomorrow we are going to say: oh, I should say this in different way. We are scientists or artist, and we are going to behave like this. If we are promoters of an already constructed reality, a view previously stablished, maybe we would be doing something different. If we are traditionalist or nationalist, and tradition or nation is already forged and embodied, the epistemological and political manufacture of reality itself is not of our concern. Fortunately, we are scientists, and this nice meeting among artist and scientist, searching for ways to rethink this world, is what makes science so attractive and useful at once. I think so.

Nango: That should be good, honestly I want to present in Japanese, 本当にそうだと思っています。"昔、男ありけり" is not "in the old days", that is not same phrase. But I want to inform something to you, I want to share with everybody.

Ogasawara: English is not taken for granted. 英語でやるのが一番いいとは思っていません。As for the relationship between several languages, the majority language has to be Japanese by the way, but we have here some Chinese or Korean speakers and Spanish speakers, Italian speakers; the all powers must be distributed as equally as possible. So we chose third language. The third language happens to be English. ずっと英語でやってきたので、例えば英語の理解が難しい方とかちょっと困ったかもしれないですけど、どうもすみません。Another reason was pragmatism, in a way. We are in short of time; a lot of people can talk a lot here and we wanted to take as many questions as possible. So I decided at some point that we should have to go with only one language. So the language issue is really important. You (public 3), you missed the afternoon session; we talked about limits of language. We consider seriously about the limits of language and that is the difference to art forms, materials, objects and everything that can be considered outside of language. But it's another impossible question, isn't it? This is the cup, but I use language to specify the material. The coffee is not inside but you can guess, nothing is dropping on but I speak, "nothing is here" in several languages. I pass the question to you as well. Because he is going to finish his PhD thesis very soon and his topic is kind of multi-lingual poetry; he is a poetry person. I admire his work on kind of multi-mystic, not only pluralised, but crossing and taking of each other kind of work. So I can understand your question, but for today, for us, the available language for our reason is English. I hope you understand that.

Public 4: I think I have a question for Nango. That's ok? I think we have talked about little contents and we also need in different way about the industrial texts. In last year we have Internet and because of the internet we have a lot of information that can be available now. I believe that the way we organize information and the way of organizing the past maybe is changing. I was wondering the last technology and science play in Internet, recording the past and organizing the past. I'm wondering if you have thought any changes that occurred specially after the Internet.

Nango: Of course the Internet is changing the world, and also the world of stories. Many short stories (are) separated through Internet, especially Twitter. First by the sled of 2ちゃんねる the short stories were spread widely. And now I think Twitter is main place for spreading short stories. Particularly in Twitter stories are too short and too simple. Of course the stories are changed in that place. Ok? 日本語で。そういう答えでよかったですか？

Public 4: 解釈の仕方とかに違いが出てるのですか。

Nango: もちろん出てます。一つの物語に対する解釈の仕方ですか。もちろん

出ていて、2ちゃんねるのスレッドで出てきた物語と、それが分解されたツイッターでの物語と、変質していっている。

Ogasawara: 多分今の質問はさっき話した archive の民主化というか、hierarchy ではなく、plural で accessibility が平等になるようになったんじゃないのっていう aspect もあるのでは。
I say, his question is something to do with democratization of archive we talked about; not hierarchical priority, you can access to any resources plurally available to you. Not really, but apparently.

Nango: ある意味ではそうなんですけど、でもやっぱりインターネットにアクセスできる層っていうのも限られている。インターネットにアクセスできる層の中を、hierarchy という言葉で表すと難しいですけど、その中には物語というものの本質をつかめる人もいれば、そうでない人もいる。でも彼らの持っている能力としては、インターネットにアクセスして情報を受けて発信することができるっていう意味での特権性もあると思います。

Ogasawara: はい。Sorry, can we leave? We are gonna close this final session. Thank you very much for your time and effort to answer to questions and comments.

Seigo Kayanoki: ありがとうございました。Thank you for everyone for joining us today and also I think you are very tired, so. Just for finishing this symposium, please give your deep clap. I think we have to thank all of students who are organizing this symposium.

All: Thank you very much.

---

1 http://archiviodiari.org/

2   Appadurai, Arjun (ed.), *The Social Life of Things: Commodities in Cultural Perspective*, Cambridge: Cambridge University Press, 1986.

言葉と記録の物質性

言葉の両義性：モノとシンボル

　シンポジウムの最後のセッションは、Part1 と 2 で行われた議論について、若手研究者二名が各々の興味関心に近づけながらコメントする、ラウンド・ディスカッションの形で行われた。すでに研究者として多くの経験を積んできた准教授や教授の巧みな論理展開だけでなく、若手の研究者が彼らに呼応するように言葉を練り出し、両者間に対話を生み出すことで、次世代へとたすきを繋げるという本来の目的に沿う議論の場となった。

　奇遇にも、発表者二人の関心には共通するテーマがあった。言葉だ。言葉が文字として表象される、あるいは意味と結合し定義される、その過程に二人はモノ／シンボルという言葉の持つ両義性を発見する。わたしたちが書籍で目にする紙面に印字された文字は、ある一定の書体の規定にならった活字として、複写技術を用いて印刷されたものだ。それは、そこに存在する、視覚されうるという意味において物質（モノ）としての性質を有している。文字の集合体としての単語、さらにその集合体としての書籍も、モノとして感知されうる。モノとしての活字の性質は、メモ用紙になぐり書きされた文字とは異なる。手書きの文字は、書き手の習慣、癖によってその都度形を異にする。要する時間の量も時と場合によって様々だ。それは身体の動きによって紙面に残される空間的かつ時間的な痕跡だと言える。百人いれば百通りの形として表れる手書きの文字。パターン化され複製されるがゆえに、一見オリジナリティを失ったように見える活字。両者のモノとしての在り方はその始まりから大きく異なる。けれども同時に、この二つは意味を表す記号として基本的には同じように機能する。他の文字と集まって言葉となり、文章を形成する。言葉の表現者となる。「明日、九時に神戸大のキャンパスで待っています」という言葉は、手書きの手紙であれ、印字であれ、あるいは、それがメールで送信されたものであっても基本的には同じメッセージを発する。言葉はこのとき、記号（シンボル）として

機能し、意味をなし、伝達する。モノ／シンボルとしてのこのような言葉の両義的な性質を理解したうえで、二人の登壇者、鋤柄史子と南郷晃子はそれぞれの観点から、記憶が言葉によって記録され、保存される、その過程そのものを再考しようと議論を展開する。そして、言葉が過去を記録する媒体として考えられる際に生じる、恣意的あるいは偶発的なずれに目を向ける。

過去を語る

　鋤柄はまず、過去に起こった、あるいは起こったと考えられている事象のなかで歴史として理解されるものと歴史の枠組みから除外されてきたものがあること、さらに歴史なるものが起こりの姿から時代の経るうちに補填されたり、一部が除去されたりして変成してきたことに触れる。そして、どのような技術によって、どんな語りのなかで歴史は歴史となるのかについて議論を展開する。建築物の例を挙げれば、メキシコシティ近郊にあるテオティワカンの遺跡の修復作業のさなかに、あるピラミッドの石段では発掘当時に発見されたよりも段数を多くするという加工が行われた。また、グアテマラとの国境付近にあるボナンパックの壁画は色を失ったモノクロの状態で発見されたが、調査をもとに描写当時の色を想定して、現存するモノクロの壁画に色が加えられた。現在、わたしたちが目にすることのできるこれらの姿は、こうした補填作業を経ている。その一方で、こうした大枠の歴史保存事業からは外れた、むしろこうしたアーカイヴィングの事業ゆえに消去される過去がある。メキシコシティの歴史地区の建物に描かれるグラフィティがそのいい例だ。鋤柄は、修復作業を主題としたあるシンポジウムで、都市空間における復元作業についての発表を聞いた。その発表者は次の問いを投げかける。メキシコシティ歴史地区の建造物に描かれたグラフィティは保存すべき記憶ではないのか、と。世界遺産にも指定されるメキシコシティの中心地は、植民地時代からの建造物が多く保存されており、政治的中枢としての役割に加えて観光産業においても重要視されている。国家や国際機関にとって優先的に捉えられる「歴史」を前に、グラフィティは単なる落書きとして始末される。バハ・カリフォルニア半島にある先史時代の岩絵は、記録すべき「歴史」として今も保存されているにもかかわらず。人類の遺産となった岩絵とメキシコシティ歴史地区で人知れず除去されるグラフィ

ティの間にある相違は、本来重層的で雑多に存在するはずの歴史が、階層化され、一元的に解釈されている現実を明確に示している。

　時間の経過のなかで行われてきたこの補填、除去という作業は、言葉の在り方にも当てはめて考えることができるのではないだろうか。時間の経過のなかで言葉もまた変容してきた。近代における科学の発展は言葉の在り方を大きく変えた。辞書では言葉が言葉によって定義される。印刷技術は書き言葉として整えられた言語を複製し、それは広範囲に流通するようになる。言葉は本来の柔軟で主体性のある性質とは異なる、客観性を備えた知識、概念として固定された生を生き始める。それはあたかも凹凸をそぎ落とし洗練されたかのように見えるかもしれない。だが実態は、標準語を作り出し、方言を周縁的なものとして区別し、話者と話者の間に分断を生んだ。それは同時に、言葉の世界を均質化し、語りを系統化する。言葉の在り方に生じたこうした変化の例として、「マヤ」という言葉を考えてみる。19世紀に西欧知識人（アマチュア考古学者、冒険家、神話学者）の間で再発見された「マヤ」は、知識として支配すべき、解読すべき他者として、そして同時に西欧という自己の過去を映す鏡として解釈された。それは、西欧にとってミステリアスで失われた過去に生きる者を指す言葉であった。古代マヤに対するアイデアは、その後ロマンティシズムやプリミティヴィズム、あるいはオカルティズムと節合し、グローバル化する時代のなかで科学的言説やメディアで語られ、加工修正されてきた。こうして構成されたマヤなるものに与えられた記号は、現代日本で語られる際にも表れる。日本語環境のなかで、しばしばマヤがいまだ解読できないミステリアスな過去として形容されることを耳にする。このように、言葉は歴史的経過のなかでその意味を編成され、解釈され、定義される。つまり、言葉は解釈の連鎖によって形作られる。言葉はその連鎖を繰り返しながら、過去を語る記号を与えられてきたのだ。

記憶、主体的な語り

　鋤柄がメキシコの事例をもとに議論を展開したのに対して、南郷は日本の古典について論じる。『伊勢物語』は平安時代の歌物語であるが、それは当時草書（くずし字）の文体で書かれた。原書は現存するものの、それは専門家や研

究者の目にしか触れられていない。一方、わたしたちは「むかし、をとこあ
りけり。ひんがしの五条わたりに、いとしのびていきけり」という文を恐らく
学校の教科書で目にし、読んできた。それは活字書体に変換されたものであり、
草書とは違ってその文字一つ一つが独立し、規則的に整えられた形をしている。
また、恐らく多くの高校生は古典の授業でその現代語訳を聞き、それが「むか
し、男があった。東の五条あたり（にある女の住む屋敷）にたいそう人目を忍
んで通っておった」などという意味であることを理解するだろう。古語の連な
りは、専門家の翻訳を介してはじめて、わたしたちにとって意味を解読できる
記号となる。

　さらに言えば、デジタル社会において『伊勢物語』について知ることは容易
で、大筋として在原業平なる男の生涯を歌っている、作者は不詳であり、成立
した年代も定かではない、今も議論が行われていることなど、ある程度の情報
を手にいれることができる。ただし、それはあくまで情報であり素材であって、
記憶ではない、と南郷は言う。もちろん、読み手がその素材を自らの経験のな
かで自らの記憶の一部として認識することは多分にあることだろう。高校の教
室で『伊勢物語』を読んでいたときに、隣にいたあの子に消しゴムを拾っても
らった。『伊勢物語』をきっかけに和歌を習い始めた。個々の実体験のなかで、
解釈は読み手にゆだねられる。このように、一方で『伊勢物語』という物語は
解釈の連鎖のなかで翻訳される。他方、草書体で書かれた原書には、書き手
の筆使いや和紙に残る染み、また和紙そのものの仕上がりや経年から語られる
はずの記憶がある。その文字は、書き手とより身体的に結びついた記憶である。
書くという作業が生むリズムは筆跡として残されている。けれども、厳重に保
管され、公開はほぼ専門家のみに限定されるという現在の環境にあって、原書
は過去を物語る資料として、記録としての価値は保証されても、主体的な記憶
を持ち続けることは可能なのだろうか。南郷は、物語はそれを語ったり、聞い
たり、読んだりする者がいてはじめて物語として生きることができると強調す
る。もっと言えば、『伊勢物語』が保存の対象となるのは、「日本の伝統」とい
う言説に組み込まれるがゆえであり、その結果、国家的な記憶、想像的な集団
の記憶なるものとして固定的な価値が付与されているのではないか。そうなの
であれば、流動的で多層的な記憶を持つモノとしての在り方は忘却され、固定

され、限定された範疇でしか生き長らえることは出来ないだろう。

　これらの問いに呼応してジャンルカ・ガッタは、物語とマテリアリティの相関的な結びつきについて論じ、別の角度から言葉が記憶として、そして同時にモノとして捉えうる可能性を示唆する。ガッタは、主体的な語りが綴られたモノ、ある年配の女性が記した日記をとりあげる。女性は日記を紙面にではなく、亡き夫と長年使用したシーツの上に記した。日記は彼女の方言で綴られ、彼女にとって親密な言葉が並ぶ。そして、その素材は彼女が長い間その上に身体を横たえたベッドシーツだ。シーツはそれ自体に記憶を抱えている。そこに彼女の主観的な言葉が綴られる。シーツと言葉というふたつのモノは、彼女という主体を介して結びつき、その記憶を語る。この例は、わたしたちが生活する日常のなかにモノの主体性が存在することを示唆する。記憶、主体的な語りは経験と強く結びついている。そしてシーツは語りが記された素材でありつつそれ自体で物語を抱える記憶なのだ。

　このセッションを、そしてイベント全体を閉じるにあたって、来館者から投げかけられたある問いに言及したい。それは、イベントで採用された言語が英語であったことへの問いかけだった。登壇者の中には、確かにイングランドやアメリカ合衆国で PhD を取得した者がいる。彼らにとって英語は自らの経験と決してかけ離れたものではないだろう。けれど、母国語として英語を話す者は一人もいない。それにもかかわらず、どうしてこのイベントでは英語が話されているのか。英語という、わたしたち個人にとって副次的な言語を通して議論が交わされ、わたしたちは何かを共有したように感じる。けれどそれは本当に互いを理解したと言えるのだろうか。議論の奥にある、より繊細な意味というのは本当に伝わっているのだろうか。

　この問いの前提として、英語がいまだにアカデミックな場で、メディアの中で、そして国際社会の場で、権威的で支配的な位置づけを獲得したままにいることを憂慮しなければならない。言語間の格差を解消することを目指していかなければならない。そしてこのイベントもまた、英語がフレイムとして機能する場となったことは確かだ。けれども忘れるべきでないのは、あらゆる言語表現はフレイミングとして作用するということ。登壇者の一人ホセ・ルイスはこ

う返答する。たとえわたしたちが日本語、スペイン語、あるいはイタリア語で話し合ったとしても、言語が考えを表現し伝達する、その手段である限り、そこには必然的に約束事が生じ、ある一定の規則が設けられる。つまり、わたしたちがどんな言語を用いて対話したとしてもフレイムは作用する。対話とはそうしたフレイミングの中にあっても自分とは異なる他者が話す言葉を理解し、解釈しようとする作業であり、同時に、他者に自己を理解してもらえるよう言葉を選ぶ作業だ。その作業では互いに互いを翻訳する。そこには誤解がつきもので、他者の言葉が含む繊細な意味を理解することは難しい。他者を完全に理解することなどできない。それでも絶え間なく対話し、理解を深めようと努力することこそ、わたしたちがこれからも続けていくことなのだ。以上の意味を込めて、本書では本文をオーセンティックな英語に書き換えることをせず、イベント時に各登壇者が発したそれぞれの英語をできるだけ残すことに努めた。一人一人が話す英語には、その発話者のリズムとトーンがある。それは、他者と対話しようと各々が発した声なのだ。(鋤柄史子)

Editors
Hiroki Ogasawara
Professor in Sociology and Cultural Studies, Graduate School of Intercultural Studies, Kobe University

Fumiko Sukikara
Ph.D student, Department of Social Anthropology, University of Barcelona

Contributors
Gracia Imberton Deneke
Professor in Institute of Indigenous Studies, Autonomous University of Chiapas, Mexico (UNACH)

Gianluca Gatta
Project Associate Professor, Institute for Promoting International Partnerships, Center for International Education - Program Coordination Section, Kobe University
Researcher for Archive of Migrant Memories, Rome, Italy

Hirotaka Inoue
Associate Professor in American Studies, Graduate School of Intercultural Studies, Kobe University

Masato Karashima
Associate Professor in Japanese Studies, Graduate School of Intercultural Studies, Kobe University

Seigo Kayanoki
Research fellow of Research Center for Promoting Intercultural Studies, PROMIS, Kobe University

Ayami Nakatani
Professor in Anthropology, Graduate School of Humanities and Social Sciences, Okayama University

Koko Nango
Research fellow of Research Center for Promoting Intercultural Studies, PROMIS, Kobe University

José Luis Escalona Victoria
Professor in Social Anthropology, Center of the Research and Advanced Study in Social Anthropology, Mexico (CIESAS)

Materialism of Archive

A Dialogue on Movement / Migration and Things
Between Japanese and Mexican Researchers

記録のマテリアリズム

移動／移民とモノをめぐる日墨研究者による対話

2021 年 3 月 25 日　初版第 1 刷発行

編者―――小笠原博毅　鋤柄史子

発行―――神戸大学出版会
〒 657-8501 神戸市灘区六甲台町 2-1
神戸大学附属図書館社会科学系図書館内
TEL 078-803-7315　FAX 078-803-7320
URL：http://www.org.kobe-u.ac.jp/kupress/

発売―――神戸新聞総合出版センター
〒 650-0044 神戸市中央区東川崎町 1-5-7
TEL 078-362-7140 ／ FAX 078-361-7552
URL：https://kobe-yomitai.jp/

印刷／神戸新聞総合印刷